Geordie Got Physical.

By Wyn Jackson.

Jackwyn.

This Book is dedicated to my
daughters Yvonne and Shelly.

Also by Wyn Jackson

Geordie Dropped In.

Jackwyn.

Published by Jackwyn

This first edition printed October 2005.
By Athenaeum Press Ltd.

Copyright @August 2004 Wyn Jackson.

Chapter 1

Mother was a polite, refined, well-spoken woman, who, as a young child, had journeyed extensively to foreign countries with her adoring adoptive mother and father, both of whom were missionaries in the Salvation Army.
Together they travelled the globe, visiting Third World countries to distribute food and clothing to the starving, impoverished inhabitants.

Witnessing the harsh poverty and lack of medical attention, together with the appalling filthy conditions which the sick, the elderly and the children had to endure, haunted mother forever.
Consequently, having been exposed to these horrors, she developed into a caring, compassionate woman and being generous to a fault, was regarded amongst our neighbours as the person who would give you her last

penny.

Mother was born out of wedlock, to a young naive, hardworking scullery maid, who at the time, was employed in a large mansion house, which was situated in the county of Durham.

A very wealthy man, namely Robert Swinburne Esquire, owned the imposing property, together with the adjoining one hundred and fifty acres of fine grassland.

This grand mansion was situated in a glorious, tranquil location, nestling in the midst of woodlands and orchards; it also incorporated a large cobbled courtyard flanked on three sides by spacious airy stables, housing the numerous horses and ponies, which were owned by members of the family.

Situated above the stables were sparsely furnished rooms, which provided lodgings for the hard working grooms and stable hands, who, even though poorly paid, were grateful for the work, and each felt fiercely loyal to their employer.

The affluent Swinburne family were heavily connected with various business concerns, mainly involving shipping lines and tea importation, each resulting in lucrative profits.

James, the handsome, suave eighteen-year-old son of Robert Swinburne, was quite a ladies' man and had quickly noticed Lilly Wainwright, a pretty, impressionable young maid who was employed in the downstairs scullery.

It was not the first time he had taken advantage of his position to seduce the female staff; he arrogantly assumed they would be fearful of losing their jobs if they refused to succumb to his advances. Lilly, his latest target, after being subtly overwhelmed by his flattery, became utterly besotted with him. One day, she, after completing her daily chores, was leaving the mansion to walk to the nearby village to visit her aunt and was gazing intently down at her red chaffed hands, wondering if they would ever be as smooth and silky as the mistress's. Suddenly, she became aware that James was following closely behind, then smiling mischievously, he stepped forward and slid an arm around her waist and guided her into a nearby barn.

Throughout the previous months, Lilly couldn't help eavesdropping when the older maids discussed their sexual exploits, so, although still a virgin and only fourteen years old, she was curious and quite fancied the idea of indulging in sexual activities herself. As James peered intently into her eyes, she found herself tingling from head to toe. He enveloped her with his arms, pulling her close and pressing his body against hers. At that moment, she became aware he was sexually aroused and although nervous, she was an enthusiastic and willing partner and was easily sweet-talked into submission. This was the first of numerous assignations in which they indulged in intercourse, so, of course the inevitable soon happened - she fell pregnant.

It was an understatement to say the least, that upon

discovering the facts, James's parents were appalled and dismayed, since being devout churchgoers, they believed if the truth became common knowledge, the disgrace and humiliation would be insufferable. Nevertheless, to give them credit, they accepted responsibility and felt it their duty to help the young scullery maid, although, she being beneath their station, marriage was not an option. However, they tenderly cared for Lilly throughout her pregnancy, allowing her free board and lodgings in one of their attic bedrooms, until finally two days after her fifteenth birthday, her labour pains started. At the onset of the imminent birth, the family duly summoned the local doctor to deliver the baby and after ten hours of agonizing labour, Lilly gave birth to a healthy fair-haired baby girl weighing seven pounds and who was subsequently named Kathleen - my mother.

To save the family from scandal and with the consent of Lilly, James's parents appealed to very dear friends of theirs, a staunch religious couple with the surname of Dodds, who, after lengthy service in the Salvation Army, had both attained the high-ranking position of Major. Mr and Mrs Swinburne asked them if they would be prepared to adopt the baby girl and since the couple had been devastated when being informed they were unable to have children of their own were delighted with the proposition and readily agreed. Therefore, after all the legalities of adoption had been concluded, they collected baby Kathleen from the mansion house and being a devoted loving couple, adoringly brought her up as if she were their own flesh and blood.

Mother was seventeen when she first encountered father. She was dressed in Salvation Army uniform and playing a tambourine with the Army band who were collecting donations outside a pub in the centre of Newcastle upon Tyne. Father, who was twenty years old, was pub-crawling with his mates and after indulging in an intense drinking session, was 'pissed as a newt' when he emerged from the pub and caught a glimpse of mother. He instantly fancied her and accordingly proceeded to 'chat her up.'

Mother's strict religious upbringing resulted in her having led a very sheltered life; therefore, being incredibly naive, she was easily taken in by father's charming 'gift of the gab' and was instantly swept her off her feet. Subsequently, to the despair of her parents, they began a relationship and were married within six months. This was truly a bizarre union; mother, a 'prim and proper,' very well spoken young lady brought up on the right side of the track, and father, an out-and-out broad Geordie rogue, albeit a loveable one.

After they married, mother and father 'lived in' with Granny Sarah who was father's mother. This was not an ideal start to the marriage, especially as Granny Sarah was a tyrant, who relentlessly bullied, intimidated and dominated mother. Shortly after their wedding, mother discovered she was pregnant, and then seven and a half months later the labour pains began. When the contractions became so severe and it became obvious mother was soon to give birth, Granny Sarah was incensed. She accused mother of having sex and becoming pregnant before marrying father. She called her a 'dirty whore,' 'a bastard' and 'a slut.' Heartlessly, ignoring mother's tearful contradictions, she, being the sadistic malicious person she was, callously threw mother out of the house. The rain was lashing down in torrents, as mother, being in the final stages of labour and doubled up in agony with the baby's birth imminent was virtually crawling along the ground on hands and knees in the direction of the hospital. She was desperate for help when exhausted and drenched through to the skin, she finally collapsed, alone and frightened, under a bush.

In the meantime father returned home from the pub and when realising his wife was not there, asked Granny Sarah, "Where's Kath?"
To which she replied,
"Aav thrown the dirty whore oot. Shi waas gaana drop the bairn, aam not haavin any bastard in my hoose"

Father frantically rushed out to trace the steps he believed mother would have taken to reach hospital and to his horror arrived upon the scene of his distressed wife, writhing about on the ground, screaming in agony. A moment or two later as father tried to console her, mother moaned, "The baby's coming."

Father was shocked when the baby's head appeared and mother, unassisted, gave birth to a daughter, who incidentally, was two months premature and weighed only two pounds, which of course disputed Granny Sarah's spiteful accusations.

A concerned passing 'Good Samaritan', upon seeing mother's predicament, immediately summoned help, and kindly waited, giving aid until the ambulance arrived to rush mother and newborn baby to Newcastle General Hospital. Upon arrival, the doctor immediately placed the tiny baby into an incubator in the intensive care baby unit. Nevertheless, he warned mother to expect the worst, informing her there was only a fifty-fifty chance the baby would survive.

The doctor reiterated he was astonished the baby, being so premature and underweight, had survived at all, especially having being born al-fresco during extreme weather conditions and moreover, without the benefit of medical attention.

Whilst mother and baby, (sister Eleanor,) were in hospital recovering from their ordeal, mother informed father in no uncertain terms, that she would never, ever, go back to live with his domineering mother. Therefore, since houses were particularly easy to rent in those days, father promptly found a dwelling. Unfortunately, it was a meagre two bed-roomed dark, damp, lower terraced house, devoid of electricity and hot water, with an outside toilet in the yard - certainly not an ideal place in which to raise a premature baby. Heaven only knows what mother's parents must have thought; their precious daughter, snatched from their luxurious residence in the 'posh' area of Jesmond, to sink to the depths of having to exist in the poverty-stricken area of Scotswood Road; however, mother was devoted to father and would go through hell and high water to stay with him.

It was three years later, on the 12th August 1934, which was a sweltering summer's day, that mother, heavily pregnant and in the advanced stages of labour, with the baby's birth pending, was once again admitted into Newcastle General Hospital.

Two hours later, at precisely 11.30.a.m, I found myself being unceremoniously dangled upside down by my ankles like a skinned rabbit; I heard a loud crack and simultaneously felt a smack on my bum, resulting in a stinging pain. A nurse carried me, screaming out in protest as loud as my little lungs would allow, to a sink filled with warm water. She gently bathed, dried and wrapped me in a soft warm sheet, then placed me into my mother's arms, all eight pounds eight ounces of me. The nurses on duty gathered around my cot cooing and fussing and asking mother if she had chosen a name for me. Mother said she was going to name me Herbert Stanley, after my father.

The nurses adamantly protested, insisting, "Eeh you can't call a beautiful little baby THAT, everyone will call him Herbie, he'll hate it." They suggested to mother that she name me Ronald, after Ronald Coleman the famous film actor, who, at that specific time, was the heartthrob of all the young women. I am pleased to say mother was persuaded to take their advice.

Three years elapsed before brother, Herbert Stanley, (father got his own way this time), made his appearance into the world. As a youngster, as predicted by the nurses, he was burdened with the name of Herbie, which he loathed. Because he despised the name so vehemently, he categorically refused to answer to Herbie and insisted everyone call him by his middle name, Stan, which to his immense relief, they did.

It was during the war, actually in the middle of an air raid in 1941, that my sister Jeanne was born, followed three years later by the baby of the family, Lilian. This completed our close-knit family.

Since our family home was very basic, and incorporated only two bedrooms, brother Stan and I were allocated one of the bedrooms, whilst sisters Jeanne and Lilian occupied the other. Mother and father slept on a bed settee in the living room and sister Eleanor slept on a bed, which was fitted into a void under the stairs.

Not having such luxury as central heating meant I shivered during the winter months, especially at night if the temperature was minus freezing and particularly when the call of nature required me to use the outside toilet. I was in the habit of pulling an old coat around my shoulders before opening the back door, then with bowed head and trembling against the biting wind, I would sprint to the outside loo. No such extravagance of toilet rolls in those days, simply a nail hammered into the back of the door, with pieces of newspapers cut to the desired size, dangling from a knotted piece of string.

Being an old house without modern amenities, the back kitchen was understandably sparsely equipped; it encompassed an old chipped sink, which sported a dark brown stain, the result of water constantly dripping over the years from the rusty tap. The kitchen also incorporated an old bath, which was concealed underneath a hinged wooden bench; however since we didn't have the pleasure of running hot water, the bath was never ever used.

Chapter 2

One of the first memories I can recall from my childhood is the day I was sitting on a huge knot, which was tied into the end of a thick rope looped around the top of the lamppost, situated outside our front door. I was nonchalantly swinging backwards, forwards, round, and round, happy as a sand boy with not a care in the world. Being only five years old, I was too young to comprehend I was attired in ragged, baggy clothes which were about two sizes too large and that I was wearing shabby second hand shoes, which had seen better days and even though father had cut out and inserted cardboard inner soles, the outer soles were so thin, I could feel every pebble and stone as I walked and played.

Suddenly I heard a weird piercing incessant sound, which bewildered me; it was a siren to warn the population of imminent enemy attack in wartime. Upon hearing the loud noise blaring out, the neighbours immediately came rushing out of their houses in sheer panic, shouting, "We're at war."

They gathered in small groups, arms gesticulating as they anxiously discussed the repercussions they believed war would bring to their lives. Apparently, the Rt. Hon. Neville Chamberlain had just made an announcement on the radio, informing the nation that, THE COUNTRY WAS AT WAR WITH GERMANY. The time was 11.15. a.m. on Sunday morning the 3rd September 1939. The atmosphere amongst the clusters of women was of disbelief and horror; then a sense of hopelessness seemed to fill the air, and even though I was so young, I realised that something was very amiss.

Our family lived in Maughan Street, which ran vertically up from the famous Scotswood Road, on which a massive factory, namely Vickers Armstrong was located. This factory was situated immediately at the bottom of our street.

Vickers Armstrong was a munitions factory which manufactured not only ammunition, but also tanks and guns which were designated for the British Army; consequently everyone believed, rightly, as it turned out, the factory would surely be a prime target for the enemy. This meant, the families being in such close proximity, would be at great risk, and likely to be caught up in any bombing raids directed against the factory.

The panic and apprehension was quite scary for me; however it turned out to be quite exhilarating and exciting for us kids in the neighbourhood. Directly the sirens sounded, we observed the urgency of neighbours extinguishing their lights or else making sure their windows were obscured with black material to conceal any lighting left on during the blackouts.

Everyone appeared to be caught up with the fear of anticipated air raids and the realisation enemy bombs would be dropping and exploding in the immediate vicinity suddenly became a reality as we huddled together in the air raid shelters. Our street was in fact, strafed several times by Nazi planes. However as soon as the 'all clear' siren sounded, we kids eagerly went out onto the streets searching for shrapnel to collect as souvenirs.

Father ushered me onto the steps outside our front door on several occasions to observe dogfights in the sky, between our Spitfires and German fighters. This was a thrilling sight. We watched as the planes dodged and evaded each other, we scrutinised the amazing spectacle of gunfire spitting out from the planes, creating bright yellow flashes, which streaked through the darkness of the night sky, virtually simulating huge firework displays.

The planes also had to contend with enormous barrage balloons, which were floating in the sky, as a deterrent to enemy aircraft. These were large, sinister grey shapes, which must have been quite daunting for pilots. In the background, we could hear the deafening noise of a huge anti-aircraft gun nicknamed Big Bertha; manned at nearby Lobley Hill and each time the enemy planes approached, it quickly came into action.

Families by their hundreds were evacuated to farms and houses situated in the depth of the countryside, the logic being, that living in such isolated, rural areas, they would be much safer and less likely to be harmed by the enemy, as primarily, the bombing targets were factories and commercial premises. Children of all ages were name-tagged, supplied with gas masks, which hung around their necks, and then were herded off to Newcastle Central Station for transportation by train to safer destinations, usually Cumberland. Older children, as a rule, would be without parents, whilst babies and younger children had the pleasure of their mothers to chaperone them. However, father refused to allow our family to be evacuated. Instead he elected we stay home, his reasoning being, "It doesn't matter where you are, when your time is up, it's up."

Father worked on and off as a coal miner, which made him exempt from enlistment into the forces, meaning he was not called up to 'Serve his Country.' Instead, he was conscripted into the Home Guard.

However, because father was rather addicted to the booze, when he was supposed to be 'on duty', he would, more often than not, be either drinking in the local pubs on Scotswood Road, or gambling in the hoying schools which used to be held in the local back lanes. These hoying schools were well patronised by local men, some of whom habitually, to the despair of their wives, gambled away all their hard earned weekly wages in just a few hours.

Inevitably the 'powers that be' discovered father was shirking his duties. I believe he must be the only person in history ever to be 'dishonourably discharged' from the Home Guard.

When I was a child, father explained to me that he was forced to 'stand to attention' while the buttons and flashes were ripped from his jacket, but because he was always an impressive joker I never did determine whether this story was true, or whether it was just another of his fabricated tales.

During the final months of the war, father was recruited into fire watching duty, and accordingly assigned to a large local grocery store, namely the Co-operative. Father was, in theory, supposed to be on 'lookout' at the store, from six. p.m., which was the time the staff departed after completing their working day and was expected to continue guard duty until seven-thirty a.m. the following morning.

Needless to say, as soon as the local pubs opened their doors at seven p.m., father, being one of their most dedicated patrons, disappeared from the Co-operative store to go boozing with his cronies. After supping Newcastle Brown until 'hoying oot' time, which in those days was ten pm, he grudgingly returned to the Co-operative store. However by this time he was generally half cut, so would find a quiet corner, to settle down comfortably and doze through until morning.

Being desperately poor meant our family had to be fed on the cheapest food, which meant mother having to purchase scraps of the most inexpensive meat, stale bread, broken biscuits and bruised fruit. Now the floodgates were unexpectedly thrown wide open; what a golden opportunity- the mind boggled with the prospect of father being let loose in a food shop. I can remember mother scribbling lists of provisions, which she gave to father, long lists which usually incorporated such items as corned beef, spam, cheese, butter, and bacon, eggs, sugar, jam, tinned fruit, milk, bread, vegetables, fruit, tea and OVALTINE. This was the first time I had ever tasted such a delicious drink and to this day, I can still envisage the aroma from the steam rising from the cup as I sipped the hot liquid savouring the flavour. After surreptitiously selecting his spoils, father would clandestinely pack the food into a cardboard box and mother would furtively creep up to the back door of the store at about six a.m., to collect the groceries before the shop assistants appeared on the scene.

Because mother's upbringing had been very religious, she felt incredibly guilty, but being a devoted mother,

Father and Mother.

we, her children, were always primarily in her thoughts, so she couldn't help but feel grateful she could at last give us something decent to eat for a change. We all took great pleasure in devouring this delicious, scrumptious food, and relished it with gratification. In hindsight, I believe we must have been the only family in the area to gain weight during those lean hard war torn times.

This help-yourself, free food continued until the war ended, then regrettably it was back to cheap poverty food; no more sumptuous feasts for us, and unfortunately no more of my favourite Ovaltine.

The extreme harsh life took its toll on mother who regrettably contracted tuberculosis, which ravaged her body until she became almost skeletal and her weight dropped to under six stones. I realised she was desperately ill, as I perched nervously on the edge of her bed gazing at her frail form she would open her eyes and a moment or two later after focusing her gaze on me would smile weakly and reach forward with her bony hand to grasp mine, I was fearful that she might not pull through as I gently squeezed her hand telling her to get better. However, I was optimistic, knowing she was a survivor and eventually my prayers were answered when, after a long haul, she eventually recovered.

However, the tuberculosis left its toll on mother and weakened by the illness, her health deteriorated so much that she was left with permanent health problems including angina, arthritis and bad circulation. As a result, her hands were always cold and blue; however she would never let her physical problems get the better of her and was always happy and cheerful.

Chapter 3

After the war, I, being the eldest son, used to accompany father almost everywhere. He usually hired a horse and cart to go hawking around the local streets and back lanes, with me, a scruffy, ragged little urchin, proudly sitting upright next to him. Father would constantly offer advice as I sat next to him on the cart. He would stress,
"Crime doesn't pay."
"Never make gold your idol."
"Don't smoke."
"Don't gamble."
"Always work hard."

Whilst his advice is permanently etched in my mind, he certainly did not practise what he preached. He drank excessively, gambled most of his wages every week, smoked like a trooper and never worked unless he was skint. However, I worshipped the ground he walked on.

Father would drive the horse and cart around the local streets, selling anything he was able to purchase cheaply, usually herring or kippers, though on other occasions it would be fresh fruit and sometimes logs.

However, if he had squandered all his money on booze, fags and gambling and was unable to buy merchandise, (which was frequently) he would just drive around the back lanes collecting rags and scrap. On arriving home, father would sort though the old clothes and any decent garments would provide clothing for myself, brother Stan and sisters Eleanor, Jeanne and Lilian.

In hindsight, I realise that, during my childhood, I never, ever, had a new item of clothing and in fact, my first brand new garment was purchased with a deposit from my first wage packet at the age of fifteen. It was a Crombie overcoat, a garment which was in fashion and all the rage at the time. My mother ordered it from a catalogue for me and I resolutely made the weekly payments until it was paid off.

When young, being exceptionally poor, we were always very shabbily dressed and on one particular day, brother Stan did not have a pair of shoes in which to go to school, so father improvised by sawing the three-inch heels off a pair of ladies' high-heeled shoes. Thankfully, Stan was too young to feel embarrassed as he skipped off to school with what appeared to be Arabian slippers on his feet, the toes of the shoes turning upwards and pointing towards the sky.

Father was a constructive man and very clever with his hands. He fashioned windmills from coloured fine plastic material and created beautiful coloured, crepe paper flowers, especially roses which he handed out to the kids who came running up to his cart with bundles of rags tucked under their arms. Father was particularly musical and won many a talent competition playing the mouth organ; in addition, he played the piano proficiently as his capable fingers skilfully pounded the keys.

It was on one of our usual hawking jaunts, when father, driving the horse and cart along Scotswood Road, spied a beautiful Italian accordion in the window of a second hand shop. The shop, which was also a pawnbroker's, was cluttered with all manner of clothing, jewellery and bric-a-brac, but the vibrant shining accordion stood out in the window like an exquisite treasure.

Father brought the horse to a standstill, jumped off the cart and gazed pensively at the accordion in the window. He noticed that the price was forty-five pounds, which of course was way out of his league. After a few minutes, he climbed back onto the cart and declared,
"If I have a good win on the horses or dogs, I will buy that accordion."

Each day, as we ambled past the shop, father slowed the horse down so he could look longingly at the accordion, dejectedly thinking his owning it would never materialise, believing it was only an unobtainable pipedream and positively out of reach.

"If only," he would muse.

One day Mrs Muir, a respected, bespectacled, middle-aged, woman, who owned the newsagent's shop on the nearby Buddle Road, requested father bring his horse and cart to clear out the flat above her shop, as the occupant, an old man, had died suddenly. Mrs Muir, being the astute businesswoman that she was, wanted to rent it out again as soon as possible. She informed father the deceased tenant had no living relatives, and suggested if he cleared out the flat, he could keep all the contents. These of course were very meagre, consisting of dusty old dilapidated furniture, shabby clothes plus a number of old miscellaneous items.

Father was unenthusiastic and extremely reluctant since he wanted to go to the pub for his usual daily drinking session. However mother began to pressurise him, pointing out that it would not take long, insisting she needed some money, seeing we had hardly any food in the house. She suggested to father that he sell the furniture to the second hand shop and even if he did not get much, a little would be better than nothing. Under extreme duress he half-heartedly agreed, and mumbled to me,

"Come on Ronnie get your coat."

Willingly, I grabbed my old threadbare coat and followed father down to the stables on Scotswood Road, where he kept his horse and cart. Over the previous weeks father had meticulously and painstakingly painted the wooden cart using all the colours of the rainbow to create beautiful bright flowers and intricate delicate motifs until finally it resembled a work of art.

Bob was a heavy type, piebald horse, having profuse white leg feathers, which matched his white mane and tail; he stood about fifteen hands high, and was a very strong willing cob. I quickly set about helping father to groom Bob by brushing him until he shone like satin. I methodically combed his mane and tail, which was so long it almost touched the ground whilst father carefully picked out Bob's feet with a hoof pick

After checking that Bob's shoes were sound, father tacked him up, fitting the polished black leather cowl around his neck, and slinging the shafts of the brightly painted cart into the side loops of the harness. Immediately this chore was completed, father and I climbed onto the cart, made ourselves comfortable on the red velvet padded bench seat, and then off we went.

Arriving at the flat, Mrs Muir presented father with the door key and we duly let ourselves in, only to be confronted with a dank fusty odour. I helped father carry the dusty old furniture down the dingy staircase, before carefully loading it onto the cart. Once this chore was accomplished, we strapped the contents securely down with a rope and climbed onto the cart. Father instructed Bob to trot on and said.

"We'll go straight home to sort these things out."

He knew that in all probability, there would be some useful household items, or maybe a few articles of clothing we could keep, and the other objects he would take to the second hand shop.

Upon reaching home, we left the heavy items of furniture strapped onto the cart whilst we unloaded the bric-a-brac, then laden with bits and pieces, we struggled into the living room to sort through what was mostly rubbish, amongst which I discovered an old brown leather Gladstone bag.

I asked. "What should I do with this father?"

"Oh! Just hoy it onto the top of the cupboard," he replied.

This I did, and was surprised when he hastily jumped up and said excitedly "Quick, get the bag back doon."

I suspected by father's eager voice there must have been something significantly important inside the bag; therefore I stood on a nearby chair, reached up, retrieved it and handed it down.

Father impatiently snatched the bag from my grasp and zealously tried to force it open. However, he found it was securely locked. He quickly turned it upside down to expose a six-inch split along the underside. Frantically, he inserted his fingers into the tear, ripped it open, reached inside and to our astonishment pulled out a wad of five-pound notes neatly rolled together and secured

with an elastic band. Father's eagle eyes had obviously seen the colour of money as the bag was travelling through the air; father impatiently ripped the elastic band from the roll and counted the money, which we assumed must have been the old man's life savings. Two hundred and seventy five pounds, a fortune to us. Father peered at me and said with a twinkle in his eye,
"You know what this means Ronnie don't you?"
I sure did, first thing next morning we hurried down to the pawnbroker's shop on Scotswood Road where father purposefully counted out forty-five pounds in five-pound notes onto the counter.

The shopkeeper was evidently puzzled as he handed over the exquisite musical instrument, probably wondering just how scruffs such as us were able to afford to buy it; nevertheless, father was now the proud owner of the Italian accordion, which he had yearned so long for. He was ecstatic and upon arriving home stated.
"Give me two weeks and I will be able to play it."

Sure enough, after practising for several hours each day, just two weeks later, he could play it as proficiently as if he had had lessons from a professional tutor. We kids assumed we were rich; two hundred and thirty pounds, we thought we would live like millionaires. However it didn't take long to dwindle away, because father being father, most of it went on drink and gambling.

Father's next scheme was to go busking in the streets

with the accordion; as I mentioned earlier, he used to take me almost everywhere so weekends were no exception. Subsequently we would walk down to the bus stop on Scotswood Road, and father with the accordion slung over his shoulder would turn to me and say,

"The very next bus that comes along, it doesn't matter where it is going, we'll jump on."

This we did, to consequently arrive at the bus's destination, which would be one of the towns or pit villages which surround Newcastle.

Father would stand and skilfully play the accordion in the streets and back lanes, with me a shabby little waif holding a cap out at arm's length for the pennies. Occasionally if we were fortunate, someone would give us two, or even three, pennies.

Father was enormously popular and wherever he played the housewives would come out from their homes, lean against their garden walls and listen to him play. They appeared to be captivated by the cheerful tunes emitting from his nimble fingers, and grateful for a moment to forget the humdrum chores of everyday life such as cleaning, washing and baking.

Father's instructions to me were always to,

"Keep counting the money and be sure to tell me when we have ten shillings."

Accordingly, every so often, I checked the money, and told him when we had obtained the goal of ten shillings, which meant that it was time to go home. I knew it would be seven shilling for father, to obtain booze and cigarettes and the other three shillings would go to mother towards housekeeping.

Another one of father's scams, which greatly amused me, was that he told fortunes. He convinced everyone in the locality he could read tea leaves. Consequently, numerous neighbours called to request his 'Services'. They all imagined he was incredibly psychic, with extraordinary telepathic powers, since father would enlighten them with details and occurrences pertaining to their personal lives, which in one way or another appeared to be accurate. Word soon spread about his 'extra-sensory prowess' until at times there would be women queuing all the way down the passage of our house, waiting to have their fortunes told. To father, being a clairvoyant was simply a joke, seeing that his 'clients' were friends or neighbours, so of course he knew many of their personal details anyway. He would say to me, "I just tell them what they want to hear, it's only common sense."

That was typical of father, anything to earn a bob or two.

Father was an extremely powerfully built man with muscular arms and shoulders and although short, being only about five feet three inches in height, despite his small stature he was one of the toughest men I have ever met. His features were very masculine and chiselled, with roguish blue eyes and despite his lack of height, he held himself proudly. I can still visualise him, when, every morning upon waking, the very first thing he did, was to fumble about for a cigarette, light up, have a drag, inhale deeply and then begin to violently hack and cough. I could never fathom out if it was the coal dust he breathed in when working down the pits or if it was it the nicotine in the cigarettes? I concluded it was probably a combination of both.

During his life, father had some dreadful accidents, some of which happened before I was born, but he, being a great storyteller would relate them me when I was a child. He told of the time, when, as a young man, he was playing in a football match and was regrettably on the receiving end of a very hard tackle. As a result, he sustained an appalling injury to his lower leg. The ensuing wound simply refused to heal and became so contaminated with infection that the hospital feared gangrene would set in, and therefore suggested amputation.

Father's mother, Granny Sarah, would not hear of it. She was adamant, and categorically refused to give permission for the surgery, and in hindsight, father was exceptionally grateful, since the wound did eventually heal, leaving him with nothing more than a scar and a slight limp.

Nevertheless, that was the end of father's football career, which was regrettable, since he, being particularly talented in that field, had previously played professionally with Exeter City. Father also had a few professional fights in the boxing ring, under the alias of George Daley; I was led to believe having an assumed name was customary in those days, probably as a tax evasion.

It was whilst working with steel erectors at a Quayside factory in Newcastle, that father fell twenty feet off scaffolding, crashing heavily onto the concrete ground below. He was rushed to Walkergate hospital by ambulance, and after examination was diagnosed as having a badly fractured pelvis, along with numerous cuts and bruises. This was a lucky escape for him as the outcome could have been very much worse; nevertheless he was hospitalised for several weeks.

One night father arrived home very late and extremely 'under the influence'. Being so paralytic he was unsteady on his feet and stumbled forward. Regrettably, as he stretched a hand out to save himself, his arm propelled straight through a glass panel in the inner door of the passage. As a result, jagged shards of glass sliced clean through an artery in his forearm and our family were horrified to witness blood pumping out with such force that it was spurting up to the ceiling. Mother panicked and screamed so loudly that a neighbour heard the commotion and came rushing to her assistance, and fortunately had the wisdom and knowledge to apply a tourniquet. Father was once again rushed to casualty to be tended by a nurse who carefully removed the slivers of glass from the wound, before gently cleaning and stitching the deep gash. Afterwards she sent him home, by now as sober as a judge.

A shocking incident experienced by father, who frequently worked underground as a miner, was one day, at the beginning of his shift, he, together with two colleagues, which was the customary number to make up a team, realised they had forgotten the jack, so father offered to return to base to collect it.

Father turned and began to retrace his steps, but after walking only about twenty-five yards, he heard a loud rumble. He swung around to glance back, and to his horror, witnessed the roof collapsing onto his work mates, instantaneously burying them under tons of rubble. Father recklessly scrambled away to locate a rescue squad and hastily guided them back to the scene to frantically help dig them out. Sadly, it was too late - they were both dead. Father arrived home some hours later and as soon as he appeared through the door, we knew immediately something dreadful must have happened, as he was ashen faced and trembling with emotion. Needless to say, he stayed off work a few weeks, until he felt he could once again face going underground.

Chapter 4

The landlord, who collected the rent every week, was a
very old man, and was so stooped in posture that he
resembled a figure seven. He sported a shock of unruly
white hair, had a scraggy long white beard and wore
spectacles with lens so thick, they resembled bottle
bottoms. He was perpetually dressed in a shabby long
black coat, which almost reached the floor, and would
shuffle up to the door in his cracked dirty leather shoes
which were worn right down at the heels. No one could
envisage why he dressed so shabbily, since he owned
most of the houses in the area and everyone supposed he
must be a very rich man.
On the days that the rent was due to be collected, father
who was usually skint, would ask in a frustrated voice,

"When is old Weazleburg (his nickname for the landlord) coming? If he doesn't hurry up I'll miss the pub."

At the time I could never comprehend why father paying the rent to Weazleburg meant he could afford to go to the pub. I only learned afterwards that father used to pay the rent with foreign money, as seemingly there was an abundance of notes around, due to servicemen bringing them home after serving abroad with the armed forces during the war.

Old 'Weazleburg' having extremely poor eyesight assumed father was giving him a pound note and since the rent was ten shillings, father received an English ten-shilling note change. Jubilant he immediately left home to go boozing in the pubs on Scotswood Road.

Brother Stan and I were 'a chip off the old block' when it came to devising moneymaking scams. Stan would sit the kids from our back lane, in a neat row along the top of our backyard wall, where, after being charged a penny, the line of ragged dishevelled little scallywags sat completely spellbound as they listened to father play the accordion. You could hear a pin drop as father, knowing they were sitting attentively, would give them a treat by playing all his best tunes.

Another moneymaking scheme was when I instructed the kids in our back lane to creep into all the neighbours' backyards, and pinch their clothes props. I encouraged them to bring the props to our backyard, where I proceeded to chop them into thin sticks as kindling after which I bound them into bundles with thin wire to sell around the doors, to the unsuspecting women whose props they had probably been in the first place. Being fair, I always made sure my helpers received an equal cut of the money.

One Saturday afternoon, I was sitting on a jetty which protruded out over the deep water of the River Tyne. I would be about eleven years old at the time and was with three of my pals, Alan Percival, Raymond Ward and Alan O'Brien.

I met Alan Percival on my very first day at school, when aged five we were both being enrolled into South Benwell School, and although Alan was the same age as myself, he towered at least a head over me and was much stronger and sturdier built than me. I was a quiet and rather shy boy; however Alan was precisely the opposite, being very confident, outgoing and extrovert. On that very first day, Alan immediately took me under his wing to protect me from a little bully called Jimmy who was intimidating me. That was the foundation of our great friendship, which lasted for many years and as boyhood chums, we were almost inseparable.

That day on the jetty, I was blissfully ignorant of my poverty-stricken appearance. There was a huge tattered hole in the front of my jumper and one of my ragged socks was hanging about two inches out from a hole in the front of my shoe. In spite of this, I was very content, and at ease with the world; the sun was shining and I had just eaten lunch consisting of bacon ends, stale bread and broken biscuits. Suddenly I was aroused from my daydreams by Alan Percival shouting,

"Last one in is a sissy."

Instantaneously, fully clothed, the four of us dived into the deep ice-cold water of the Tyne. It was at that precise moment that I recollected learning how to swim, which was at our local Bond Street swimming baths.

I was just eight years old on that first visit to the swimming pool, and was chaperoned by my elder sister Eleanor, who was eleven years old and already a proficient swimmer. It was an afternoon during the summer school holidays, and I was unaware of the bizarre spectacle I must have made, as not being able to afford to buy me a 'proper' bathing costume, my father had contrived to make one for me. My 'bathing costume' was concocted from an old brightly patterned thick woollen jumper; father removed the sleeves to create leg openings and then sewed the neck opening to conceal my modesty, after which, he stitched elastic around the hem of the jumper to form the waistband.

Oblivious of my outlandish appearance, I proudly strutted from the changing rooms towards the pool to contemplate my next move. I was nervously perched at the edge of the baths, gazing at the blue rippling water, unaware I was standing at the deep end, when unexpectedly, Eleanor rushed forward and recklessly pushed me into the water. As I submerged, the weight of the water stretched my 'bathing costume' down past my knees exposing my willie. Consequently being unable to swim I was floundering and panicking, whilst at the same time, trying to pull my 'bathing costume' up to cover my modesty. Eleanor stood at the side of the pool and was in stitches, but after a moment, when I sank to the bottom of the pool, she realised, to her horror, I was in dire trouble, so swiftly dived in and pulled me out. I was retching and spluttering as I gasped in mouthfuls of air and felt as if I had swallowed half the pool.

This experience made me determined to learn to swim, so each morning during the rest of the school holidays, I ran errands for neighbours to earn cash and gathered pop bottles to return to shops and claim the deposit. After earning the pennies, which were required for the entrance money, I attended the swimming baths every afternoon until eventually; I could swim like a fish.

Back to that Saturday afternoon, when dripping wet from our swim in the River Tyne, as Alan I walked up Maughan Street we noticed several women chatting in their front gardens, patiently waiting for their husbands to come home from the pubs, most of whom would invariably be inebriated.

It was not long after, that our next-door neighbour, Charlie Watson, came staggering unsteadily up the road, and upon reaching his house, he immediately slumped down onto the doorstep in an intoxicated stupor. His head flopped down onto his chest, his arms hung loosely by his side, his legs were askew as he instantly fell asleep and began to snore loudly. Katie, his wife, who had a passion for a tipple herself, was waiting, incensed he was an hour late for the dinner she had been 'slaving over a hot stove' cooking for him. Therefore as soon as Charlie flopped to the ground, Katie started to remonstrate with him. She began to curse and swear, but Charlie seemed to be oblivious to her ranting and raving, since he completely ignored her.

This infuriated Katie, who was so enraged that she stormed into the house, grabbed a handful of dinner plates, came back out and stood towering over Charlie, and then she systematically smashed the plates one by one onto his head, screaming obscenities with each one.
"You f—g bastard." - SMASH "You drunken whoremaster" - SMASH "You've slept with that f--—g barmaid haven't you?" SMASH.

Charlie numbed by the drink, did not appear to feel the pain, but slowly lifted his head, to focus his bleary eyes on Katie and said in a drunken slur.
"What yer deeing that fer, Aav niver dun anythin wrang."

The neighbours casually glanced at the commotion; which was nothing out of the ordinary, as drunken clashes were a common occurrence in the street. If it were not one family feuding then it would be another, especially at weekends.

Drink seemed to rule the lives of most families in our area in that period, and it was the next Saturday afternoon that a neighbour summoned a police officer to our street to arrest an aggressive drunk who was standing in the middle of the road shouting obscenities and

38

waving his arms about challenging everyone in sight to fight. Upon arriving at the scene, the police officer promptly handcuffed the drunk's wrist to his own and began to walk the short journey to the nearest police box, but just as they were passing our house, the drunk without warning threw a left hook, which knocked the police officer unconscious and he immediately slumped to the ground. However, the drunk continued walking, and since they were still handcuffed together, the comatose police officer was being unceremoniously dragged along the ground behind the drunk who was quietly muttering oaths. Each time the police officer attempted to stand up, the drunk whacked him once again. This continued until another two police officers rushed to the rescue; however, it took all three, using all their strength, to restrain the intoxicated man who was duly arrested and transported to the police station.

Another incident, which made me laugh, was, when another chap was so under the influence of alcohol that he could not walk, so he painstakingly crawled on hands and knees from the pubs on Scotswood Road making his way up the whole length of our street but every so often he would collapse onto the pavement and have a short snooze. Eventually, after managing to drag himself to his feet he noticed the knees of his trousers had disintegrated into large tattered holes and the turn-ups were worn to shreds. Staring down in disbelief, he slurred. "Ee what's happened to me troosers? The wife'll gan mad; it's me new suit, it's the forst time on- ee she'll kill is."

39

Then there was old Jim, another habitual daily visitor to the pubs on Scotswood Road, Jim was in his seventies and nothing but nothing would keep him from his daily booze up - he would, without fail, visit the pub, come rain or shine. One winter's day, in the year of 1947, the whole area was completely snowbound after several inches of snow had fallen overnight and since the winds were strong and blustery, the snow had been whipped up to form drifts several feet high so most people had to dig their way out of their houses.

The regular drinkers in The Gun, which was a pub managed by Seaman Tommy Watson, who was ex. British Featherweight Boxing Champion, agreed amongst themselves,

"Old Jim definitely won't make it today."

However shortly afterwards, to everyone's astonishment, Jim appeared through the door with a shovel tucked under his arm. This caused great amusement when he explained he had used the shovel as a sledge, by sitting on it and holding the handle in front as a rudder, one goal in mind, the pub and Newcastle Broon. How he negotiated the death-defying journey, hurtling down a sheer precipitous street, beggars belief.

Chapter 5

Now, when in pensive mood, I reminisce about the innocent 'adventures' we experienced as boys, such as the instance when one of our school teachers was reading out aloud to the whole class, the classic story of Tom Sawyer and Huckleberry Finn. We would be about ten years old at the time and the story enthralled us. We sat listening intently to their adventurous escapades, which put ideas into our heads. After school, Alan and I, together with another three boys from our class, devised a plan, which was to creep out of our respective beds that night, while our parents were asleep and to congregate at the top of our back lane at midnight.

From there, the five of us quietly crept the mile to the local cemetery, St James's Churchyard. I recall the night in question was particularly spooky, the sky hung with low heavy clouds, which entirely obscured the stars and moon, resulting in an eerie purplish darkness. To make matters worse it was particularly windy.

Trying to sport brave faces, but feeling anything but, the bunch of us carefully crept into the graveyard, each one trying to panic the other by secretly throwing small pebbles and whispering, "What's that?" or asking, "Did you hear that?"

However, we only managed to scare ourselves.

We wandered through the cemetery, gingerly picking our way past headstones and monuments. The trees were swaying and rustling noisily in the howling wind, their branches creaking and bending almost to breaking point, leaves were scuttling around our feet as our imaginations went into overdrive. We were all truly petrified but would not admit it. All of a sudden Alan pointed and shouted, "Look."

To our horror, we saw a white shape, which appeared to be floating towards us; we were riveted to the spot with fear.

"It's a ghost," Alan whispered.

With that, we spun around and took to our heels, running as if our lives depended on it. We made a beeline for the small stone wall surrounding the graveyard, which was about two feet high and physically threw ourselves over. However, we were traumatised to find ourselves falling from a height of about six feet;

unbeknown to us, the ground was at a much lower level on the other side. Consequently, we ended up in a heap, falling one on top of the other; fortunately for us, a mound of sand helped to soften our fall. We picked ourselves up, and as we dusted ourselves down, we glanced up and to our alarm; the 'ghost' appeared at the top of the wall. We were trembling with alarm, when the hazy white form leaped at us. It was only then that we realised it was a large white dog.

Another day, during summer school holidays, again whilst I was about ten years old, a youth called Thomas Corkhill, who was in fact several years older than me, said, "I've got a great idea."

That idea was to arrange a boxing 'Championship Show,' setting up contests by matching the boys from our street, against boys from the adjoining streets. "The Champion," he said, "will win sixpence prize money." Sixpence! My mind went into overdrive - sixpence could buy a bar of chocolate and I could go to the pictures to see a film. Then I slowly came down to earth when I realised that sixpence would buy a loaf of bread for my mother. The 'boxing' began at ten o'clock in the morning, and continued until all the boys had been eliminated, all that is except my pal Alan O'Brien and myself. We had both fought on and off all morning having had numerous 'fights' until we had ultimately won through to the "final."

The deciding contest began immediately after lunch,

when Alan and I donned the gloves to start our contest. Incredibly, this 'fight' lasted until four o'clock in the afternoon, Corkhill egging us on, insisting we continue even when flagging and showing signs of tiredness.

Driven on by the promised prize money Alan and I fought as if our lives depended on it.

"Just a few more rounds," Corkhill shouted.

Finally, after three hours of so-called boxing, we were so fatigued that we could hardly lift our hands and then both downright disappointed when Corkhill declared the contest.

"A DRAW," and said

"Because there is no outright winner, neither of you gets the sixpence."

Not only were we utterly exhausted, but enormously frustrated to say the least. The mean bastard could easily have split the prize money and given us three pence each.

My next experience, which was especially daunting, was at 'The Bog', a favourite play area for most of the kids in the neighbourhood, it being the site of a derelict abandoned brickwork's factory. The attraction of the vicinity was obvious, especially for boys since The Bog was located on the north bank of the Tyne, and had a broken-down jetty protruding out into the river, which we kids used as a diving board. There was a thick rope Tarzan swing and an abundance of open space in which to kick a ball around. Therefore, many of the local kids would spend hours playing happily at the location, especially during school holidays and weekends.

Also situated at the site was an obsolete drift mine which had in the past been a working coal pit. The access had been at ground level which meant the miners, in their day, walked straight into the pit instead of having to go below ground by lift. In an earlier period when the mine was abandoned, the entrance had been bricked up by the N.C.B. However over the years the bricks had eroded so much, they had crumbled away to create a small opening into which a child could climb.

One afternoon I made my way to the drift with brother Stan. I was about twelve years old at the time and Stan would be nine. We went prepared with two sacks, an axe, a candle and a box of matches. The intention was that we would hack coal from the old seams, bag it, then sell to our neighbours, thus earning a little pocket money.

Upon arriving at the drift, Stan and I crawled through the opening, lit a candle and crept down a tunnel which was to lead us to a large round area called the wheelhouse, appropriately named since it was circular in shape with numerous tunnels branching off in all directions. I selected a specific tunnel at random and we started to walk through. Unfortunately after a short time, the flame of our candle suddenly extinguished.

We tried numerous times to re-light it in vain, and then discovered we had run out of matches. At that point, neither of us was too concerned, and began to gingerly grope our way in complete darkness, back to the wheelhouse. However, upon arriving there, I unfortunately could not for the life of me remember which tunnel would lead us to safety. Although beginning to feel nervous I didn't want to panic Stan so put on a brave face, and tried to reassure myself by saying, "Keep calm, be methodical."

We began to slowly and systematically fumble our way down one tunnel after another, stumbling about in total darkness, but to no avail.
Now the terror started to creep in when realising we were indeed, hopelessly and utterly lost. Stan by now was reduced to quietly sobbing to himself and I being the 'big brother' was myself beginning to feel, beyond doubt, petrified. I was full of desperation and my confidence slowly ebbed away when gradually grasping the gravity of our situation. Realising that we hadn't informed anyone of our plans and knowing we would not be missed, the warm tears began to run slowly down my face.

It was hours later when desperately crawling along yet another pitch-black damp tunnel, feeling confused and disorientated, with Stan hanging onto the hem of my coat for dear life, I spied a tiny pinprick of light in the distance. I was euphoric when I realised it must be daylight which would subsequently lead us to safety. I shouted. "Look Stan, look; it's the opening to the

46

outside."

We scrambled towards it crying and laughing at the same time, then as we neared the light we could feel the fresh air on our dirty faces, which were by, now streaked with tears. We felt exhilarated with relief as we clambered outside and once safe we realised to our horror that we had been lost inside the drift for four long hours.

What makes this story more horrific is the fact two weeks after our terrifying ordeal, another two local boys, James Quinn and George Derek who lived in nearby Sutton Dwellings and who were both about the same age as myself, had the same idea as Stan and me, and went into the drift to pick coal. The date was the Thirtieth of January 1947. However after several hours the boys failed to emerge and were subsequently reported missing. Rescue squads were quickly summoned to locate them, but unfortunately, by the time, they found them, which was not until the Fifth of February, they had sadly perished. I could not help thinking. 'There but for the grace of God go I'.

This tragedy prompted the NCB to make sure that no-one could ever enter the drift again by bricking up the entrance so securely it would be impossible to penetrate to gain access. Not that I or brother Stan would ever have wanted to - no, never, ever again.

The headmaster of my school, South Benwell, was a

Mr Tweddle, who, although an extremely strict disciplinarian was in fact a very fair and just man. During lessons, he would creep around the school, peeping through the glass partitions which separated the classrooms and if he so much as spied a boy misbehaving, or even chatting, he would silently and stealthily sneak up, grab him by an ear, then practically holding him up in mid air, would march the guilty culprit on tiptoes directly to his room, at which point the boy would receive a rigorous lashing with the belt.

Eddie Scott was the typical school troublemaker who was primarily the instigator of all the rebelliousness in our class; as a result, our form teacher Mr Drake positioned Eddie in the desk immediately in front of his own, meaning he could keep the scoundrel under close observation. One day during the first week of November, Eddie came to school armed with a firework concealed in his pocket. The firework described as a Cannon, was a thunderously loud banger.

Mr Drake, in addition to being our English teacher, was a local magistrate, and much respected and well liked by the pupils, consequently during his lessons, the atmosphere was so silent you could almost hear a pin drop. That morning, half way through the English lesson, Eddie furtively lit the Cannon and covertly rolled it under Mr Drake's desk. A split second later it exploded and being in such a confined space, the blast was thunderous.

Mr Drake jumped about two feet into the air with shock, and knowing whom the culprit was sure to be, grabbed Eddie on the way down, pulling him out of his seat by the lapels of his coat, and shook him like a rag doll. A split second later, the headmaster Mr Tweddle came storming into the smoke filled classroom, demanding to know what had caused all the commotion and noise. Upon discovering the facts, Eddie was frogmarched to his office, to receive his physical chastisement, a severe trouncing with a belt.

A few weeks later, there was another incident. This was when another pupil in my year, Davy Nixon, was being especially intolerable to Mr Morgan our form master. Davy was being very obnoxious and was ignoring and defying Mr Morgan, who was trying his utmost to reason with him.

Uncharacteristically, Mr Morgan, who was such an inoffensive teacher, suddenly lost his cool and in frustration, retaliated by slapping Davy across the face. Taken completely by surprise, Davy immediately ran from school, heading home. We other pupils knew exactly what would happen, and waited with bated breath.

Sure enough, as anticipated, about twenty minutes later, the outer door burst open with a resounding crash. We heard heavy footsteps, clump, clump, clump approaching, nearer and nearer, louder and louder. A few seconds later, our classroom door burst open. CRASH, the noise reverberated through the classroom. Davy's mother, Mrs Nixon, who was dragging him alongside by his arm, strode purposefully up to Mr Morgan. Planting her feet toe to toe with his, she screamed in his face "Did yee hit im?"

As Mr Morgan was meekly trying to explain that Davy had deserved to be chastised, suddenly without warning, Mrs Nixon threw a right hand punch Rocky Marciano would have been proud of. The blow landed bang on target, Mr Morgan's chin, knocking him clean out of his chair and into a crumpled heap on the floor. As he lay dazed, spectacles askew, mouth gaping open, he could only watch in disbelief as Mrs Nixon strutted out of the classroom, slamming the door behind.

Another of our teachers, Mr Brown, had formerly been a sea captain in the navy, and had a novel way of disciplining his pupils. His favourite method of punishment was to stand the offending boy behind the swivel blackboard and continue with the lesson. However, if he thought that the pupil was misbehaving behind his back, he would sporadically flip the blackboard onto the offender's head. It soon became a contest between the pupil and the teacher - who had the quickest reaction? Could the pupil dodge out of the way in time? We noticed it was not very frequent.

One morning a pupil named Billy Chapman was being very badly behaved, which of course was nothing unusual for boys of fourteen. He was duly chastised, and as usual, ordered to stand behind the blackboard. Whilst there. Billy began to grimace and contort his face so horrifically, he could quite easily have won a gurning competition. In addition, he was making frantic two fingered gestures at Mr Brown from behind the screen of the blackboard. Upon hearing the class sniggering, Mr Brown realised Billy was playing silly beggars, so nimbly flipped the blackboard. However Billy was so intent on making signs, he didn't observe it and was therefore caught a glancing blow on his head. This enraged Billy so much, he promptly grabbed the bottom of the blackboard with both hands and threw it up with all his strength. Consequently it clobbered Mr Brown, with full force on the top of his head.

Almost knocked unconscious, Mr Brown staggered forward, and wobbled across the room. The rest of the class could sense that he was filled with rage, so fearing repercussion, we were biting our lips, too terrified to laugh as knowing if we did, we would face his wrath. Understandably Billy's punishment was a severe thrashing with the belt.

A group of boys in my year, led as customary by Eddie Scott, decided 'enough was enough.' Why should they, the pupils, suffer the humiliation of corporal punishment? Accordingly they put their heads together to devise a plan, which was to steal the teachers' belts. They patiently waited until lunchtime, and whilst the pupils and teachers were enjoying their meal, each boy chose a classroom, and then individually they crept furtively into their designated room and nicked the belt from within the teacher's desk.

The gang, each with his spoils concealed within his clothing, advanced to the cloakroom, whereupon they proceeded to cut the leather belts into tiny pieces and subsequently flush them down the toilets. All, that is, with the exception of one boy, who had hidden his belt, without the knowledge of the others, behind a cupboard in one of the classrooms. That very afternoon, the group of boys deliberately began to antagonise our teacher by misbehaving and being extremely loud and obnoxious. It did not take long before Mr Brown exploded with fury, and ordered the six teenagers involved to "Get out here at once."

They strolled casually towards him, smirking knowingly to themselves, and as they lined up in front of him, he angrily opened his desk and reached inside for the belt, but of course, it was not there. He hollered to one of the boys,

"Go to Mr Drake and borrow his belt."

This of course was a fruitless journey,

"Go to Mrs Bell and get hers."

Another wasted trip,

"Go to Mr Havis."

"Sorry sir, he can't find his belt."

At this point, he concluded that something was wrong, so ordered one of the pupils to,

"Go and get Mr Tweddle."

The headmaster, Mr Tweddle, upon being informed all

the teachers' belts were missing, was enraged to say the least. His face turned scarlet, his eyes widened and were almost popping out of his head. He ranted and raved to the point that he was almost pulling his hair out with rage.

Since he was not able to extract any satisfactory answers from his questioning of the boys, as they were staunchly tight-lipped, he sent for the law. Within a short time, a large burly, round faced police officer arrived at the school, which scared the living daylights out of the culprits, who now realised they were in genuine trouble. At first, the boys emphatically denied any knowledge of the missing belts, but one by one after intense interrogation, they crumbled and confessed, pleading it was only a prank that had gone wrong.

The one surviving belt was immediately retrieved from behind the cupboard, and was used overtime on the perpetrators by Mr Tweddle. The rest of the pupils heard him administering the punishment and this in itself served as a warning to the rest of us.

It was during this period that I would 'weigh up' the boys at school, and try to predict who would do well in the future, and which boys would turn out to be no-good villains. Although there were several scamps in my class, I believed their pranks were merely the results of high spirits and omitted them from my 'list' of rogues.

My forecasts proved to be correct, when several years later, as I had envisaged the six worst troublemakers in the school, who were a year older than me, upon reaching the ages of sixteen and seventeen and being too lazy to work, spent most of their leisure time committing crimes, including theft and burglary. They progressed to perpetrating gang rapes, muggings and gay bashing, about which they openly bragged.

If they crowed about their crimes within earshot of myself, I would look upon them with contempt, and confront them, saying they deserved to be caught, and it would only be a matter of time before they were.

That day eventually arrived, when after a particularly vicious assault, having unmercifully beaten and kicked a guy about the face and head, before stealing his wallet, watch and rings, so ferociously in fact, as a result of his injuries he lost the sight in one eye. The local press reported it as the worst case of violence ever seen on Tyneside. Fortunately, they perpetrators were caught red-handed by the police with the stolen articles in their possession. This overwhelming evidence incriminated them without any question of doubt, and each was sentenced by the court, to eight years in prison.

They served six years before their release.

Chapter 6

Overall, I would say my school days were especially happy, with the exception of one particular period in which I was methodically and callously bullied. I was eleven years old at the time.

The bullying commenced when a group of lads merged together to form a gang, of which the ringleader was a boy in my class called Skinny Watson. I was soon to discover, to my dismay, that I was the gang's main target and every time they caught sight of me, they not only verbally taunted me, but also ruthlessly physically abused me. Whenever they encountered me, they gathered around to form a circle then punched and head butted me until I fell to the ground, thereupon they proceeded to kick me while I lay curled up motionless.

Consequently I regularly arrived home bruised, bleeding and crying.

Mother used to hug and comfort me, but father would chastise me saying,
"Stop being a cry baby, stick up for yourself. If you can't hit them, kick them. All bullies are cowards; hurt them and they will run a mile."

It was on yet another day, when going home for lunch the gang of five lads attacked me once again. They heartlessly knocked me to the ground, and then took turns to run at me to put the boot in. I heard them shout "Gan on Skinny, kick him in the heed."

Being egged on, he ruthlessly obeyed, booting me repeatedly, until I nearly lost consciousness. My head was swimming and I felt dizzy and sick, their voices became fainter and fainter and I did not even feel the pain of the last few kicks. Thankfully, I heard a voice, which seemed to come from a distance, which said,
"Pack it in Skinny, he's had enough."

Mercifully, the kicking ceased and the gang ran away. After a moment or two, I gingerly picked myself up, and through the throbbing pain, I decided enough was enough. I remembered father's advice and dragged myself home. I grabbed his reinforced pit boots and pulled them on and by then I had almost recovered and was in a blinding rage and determined to put an end to the bullying once and for all. I hurried back to school and laid in wait for the bullyboy Skinny Watson.

Knowing where he lived, I was aware of the exact direction from which he would return to school. Therefore I concealed myself around a corner, furtively waiting. In due course Skinny Watson came into view, swaggering back to school; his strutting posture seemed to shout out "Look at me I'm the leader of the gang."

However as soon as he emerged from around the corner, I stepped out to confront him. He reeled back in surprise, not quite the big bully without all his mates. I set to, and laid into him and gave him the biggest hiding of his life. I kicked him as hard as I could, repeatedly, until he was crying for clemency and mercy.

I have never ever condoned violence, so was not proud of my actions, but the outcome was that my retaliation sorted my predicament out, and from that day on, I was never ever picked on, or ever bullied again. I was in fact, respected by the rest of the boys. The four other members of the gang stayed away from school for several days; I could only assume they were frightened they would receive the same punishment that I had meted out to Skinny. However when they eventually came back to school, they all sheepishly apologised to me and asked me to join their gang. I vehemently declined as there was no way I wanted to be associated with gangs or bullies.

This experience made me determined to be able to defend myself properly, so I decided to join Grainger Park Boys Club to learn the art of pugilism.

I was soon to discover however, that enrolling into Grainger Park Club was not that simple. I arrived at the club, clutching the two shillings and sixpence joining fee which father had given me, only to be taken aback when confronted at the door by a prefect.

"How old are you?" he asked,

"Eleven," I replied

"Sorry you are too young, and anyway there is a long waiting list for membership."

I listened with disbelief, and was bitterly disappointed, but my determination would not let it stop there. From then on, I persisted and pestered and for three weeks, every single night, rain or shine I walked the three miles to the club, grasping my two and sixpence. Upon arriving at the door, I pleaded and begged with the prefect to allow me to join, then at last, one night out of sheer exasperation, he said, "Wait there."

He left me standing on the threshold and disappeared into the club to discuss the issue with Skipper Teasdale, who was the founder member and leader. Skipper Teasdale was greatly revered by all members, as he had saved many a youth from a life of crime by keeping them off the streets, and out of mischief. Skipper had strict rules; amongst which were that if anyone convicted of, or even suspected of being involved in any criminal offence would immediately be expelled from the club.

The prefect informed Skipper of my perseverance, and diligence, telling him I was turning up on the doorstep every single night without fail. Skipper Teasdale must have felt some compassion towards me because he instructed the prefect to admit me into the club. Once inside. Skipper enquired why I was so keen to join, I replied, "I want to learn how to box, to protect myself from bullies."

Skipper pondered for a moment then conceded by allowing me to join, but reiterated, that I was too young to box, and he would only allow me to watch the schoolboys train.

That first night I was spellbound as I observed the young boxers training. I watched intently, absorbing all the moves, and was captivated by the evasive actions, the bobbing and weaving, the footwork and the various different styles of boxing, from that night on, I made it my resolution, one day I would be better than any of them.

Being a determined little so and so, it was just two weeks later that I realised watching was not enough to satisfy my desires, so once again I nagged and nagged Skipper, "Please let me join in the training, PLEASE Skipper."

He must have been thoroughly exasperated with me because eventually he agreed to allow me to join in the training sessions. I was elated and trained religiously five nights a week and three times every Sunday.

Each member was proud to be associated with Grainger Park Club, believing it to be the best gym on

Tyneside. In addition to being kitted out with a brand new modern gym and also the best boxing equipment, it encompassed three showers. Consequently, not having the pleasure of running hot water at home, at the end of every training session I took advantage of this luxury. I revelled in the sensation of hot water raining over my body as I lathered myself with soap provided by the club. I washed away the perspiration and grime and experienced a feeling of warmth and cleanliness; I had never felt as hygienic in my whole life.

Subsequently, after learning the art of boxing and achieving a high level of physical fitness, the first fight of my amateur boxing career was duly arranged. This was in the first round of the schoolboy championships and the contest was to be held in Middlesbrough Town Hall.

I arrived home from the club extremely excited and told mother that Skipper had arranged my first fight. Her face crumpled with panic; she was alarmed that I, her little boy, might sustain an injury. I tried to assure her I would be perfectly safe, and was thrilled and excited with the thought of travelling away from home, even though Middlesbrough is only about forty miles from Newcastle. However as an eleven year old, who had never travelled outside the immediate area, it could just as easily have been Lands End.

The contest was due to be held on a Saturday afternoon, and I recall my mother leaving home early that same morning to catch a bus into the centre of Newcastle. Her destination was an outside market named Paddy's Market; she was armed with her purse and enough money to buy me a pair of second hand shoes, "To make you look more presentable," she said,

Paddy's Market was exceptionally popular, and held every Saturday morning on the Newcastle Quayside. It consisted of row after row of wooden tables and stalls, which sold second hand clothes and shoes.
The market was always teeming with mothers, young and old who could not afford new clothes for their children, so would eagerly sift through piles of clothes searching for bargains, which they invariably found. Mother rummaged around to find and buy me a pair of black laced up leather shoes, which were almost new. She hurried home and asked me to try them on. I found they were slightly too big but when I wore two pairs of socks, they were fine. I hastily dressed, walked to the club and clambered aboard the bus which had been hired to transport the boxers and trainers to Middlesbrough.

This first fight I narrowly lost on points, but to the relief of my mother I did not come to any harm. That was the beginning of an extremely busy amateur career, during which I had approximately one hundred fights, winning ninety-five per cent. My life was extremely hectic with up to three or four contests a week and occasionally, during competitions, I even boxed three times in one day.

My father was very proud of me, but regretfully, I have to admit, when he was drunk he was an out and out pest. When I was twelve years old and doing particularly well in the ring, he would sometimes bring several of his paralytic cronies to our house after chucking out time from the pub.

I was usually asleep in bed after coming home exhausted from the gym, but unfortunately father would insist that I get up, "To give an exhibition," for his intoxicated pals.

We had two pairs of boxing gloves and father would be adamant, insisting I pull one pair on, and he would don the other. Kneeling down on the floor, in front of his drunken mates who were slouched on the chairs and settee to make up the audience, father would slur, "C'mon, show em ow gud yi are."

Then he would whack me with a left hook and sticking his chin out, say. "Gaan on stick one on there."

Then he gave me another thump.

"Show em yer left." Another clout.

I would not retaliate; I just stood feeling self-conscious and embarrassed.

This scenario happened numerous times over the next few months, and I was beginning to feel more and more aggravated each time. Then one night I was so annoyed at father's taunting and teasing, I saw red and reacted.

As he stuck his chin out, goading me and inciting me to hit him, I threw my right hook as hard as I could which hit him full in the face. Father toppled over onto the

Eleven years old.

floor, then using his elbows to push himself upright, he began to spit teeth out, first one then another then a third. I was horrified and nervously awaited his reaction. I expected him to be furious, but he sat erect, blood dripping from his mouth and with a proud grin on his face, drunkenly slurred to his cronies "What'da tell ya, he'shh brilliant."

Thankfully, he did not put me through the humiliation ever again.

The first time Granny Sarah came to a venue to see me box, was after I had reached the finals in the N.A.B.C. This contest was against a junior from Hexham and was for the Northumberland Junior Championship title.

These championships were held at the famous New St. James' Hall, Newcastle and that night the hall was full to capacity with four and a half thousand spectators. When the bell rang to commence my bout, I immediately went into action and this paid off because I knocked my opponent out within one and a half minutes of the first round. I felt elated and euphoric in the knowledge I was now NORTHUMBERLAND CHAMPION. I felt as if I was walking on air as I made my way up the aisle towards the dressing rooms. However, as I walked past Granny Sarah who was sitting at the end of a row, she leaned over, reached out and grabbed my elbow. I expected her to congratulate me and to say, "Well done Ronnie."

However, what did I get -?

"Hu! Ah cud iv knocked him oot meesell."

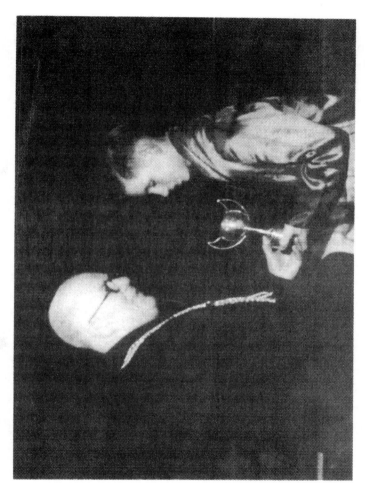

Winning the Northumberland Championship.
Cup presented by the Lord Mayor of Newcastle.

Talk about being deflated, I was certainly brought down to earth with a wallop, but to give her a little credit she did congratulate me later.

Chapter 7

Granny Sarah was a formidable woman. She was of tiny stature, was stoutly built and wore silver-rimmed spectacles, which were always perched halfway down her nose. She would peer over them and her piercing eyes would send shivers down my spine. Her grey hair was always neatly pulled back and tied into a bun at the nape of her neck; she had unusually large hands, which were red and callused. She could undoubtedly be described as a woman of dual personality, since one minute she could be kind and helpful and the next, violent and obnoxious.

Every Sunday afternoon, it was customary for us, her grandchildren, to be invited for tea; therefore my brother, sisters and I would arrive at her house at three o'clock.

Upon arriving, one of us would gingerly take the highly polished brass knocker and lightly knock on the front door and patiently wait on the doorstep until we heard the clump clump of her footsteps walking down the passage. She would vigorously throw open the door, peer over her glasses and shout.
"Cum in and sit doon."

As we tentatively entered the living room, the black cast iron stove would be roaring full blast and the heat would almost bowl us over. The aroma of freshly baked bread would envelop us, as trays of freshly kneaded bread were sitting in neat rows on the hearth and on the mantelpiece. Each tray was covered with a spotlessly clean tea towel, waiting for a batch of golden bread to come out of the stove before it was their turn to be baked. We would sit on the sofa; eyes cast downward, petrified, shaking in our boots, not daring to speak, knowing Granny's mottos were, "Children should be seen and not heard." and "Speak when you're spoken to."

Granny was very proficient with her culinary skills, and the food she served up to us was home made. In addition to crusty bread, there would be soup, sandwiches and cakes which were particularly scrumptious, being filled with home made jam and thick cream. After feasting our faces, we would politely say "Thank you, Granny, see you next week," before leaving for home.

Granny Sarah lived in a terraced house, which shared a back yard with an upstairs neighbour. One day, she was in the yard hanging clothes out to dry, when the man who lived in the neighbouring house came staggering and reeling into the yard. He was as drunk as a skunk and instead of using the outside toilet; he promptly urinated against the wall in full view of Granny.

Granny was livid and stotting mad. She confronted him and gave him a severe tongue-lashing, screaming at the top of her voice, "You dirty f—g bastard, if ah had a knife aad cut the f—g thing off."

There is no doubt; she certainly would have tried if there had been a knife within reach. This incident became an obsession with her. She dwelt on it day and night, and swore to get retribution on the "dirty bastard."

However, a week later, she contracted pneumonia and became extremely ill. Her doctor made an emergency call and after administering treatment, he advised the family to move her bed over to the open window so she could breathe some fresh air into her lungs.

It was later that afternoon, the drunken culprit walked past her window. How she summoned the strength, no one could comprehend, but she somehow managed to drag herself out of her sick bed, throw herself through the open window and begin to attack him. Finally, utterly exhausted by the effort and weakened by her illness, she collapsed in a heap at his feet. This proved the calibre of the woman; practically at death's door but revenge was utmost in her mind.

On one occasion, after receiving reports that a Peeping Tom was lurking in the vicinity, as the pervert had been observed several times crouching beneath house windows peering inside, the police gave out a warning to all residents in the area to be on their guard. However, Granny had the perfect solution, "Just let the bastard dare cum to my hoose. He'll get what he thoroughly desorves." she said.

She purposefully set aside a large pan of water, which she kept at boiling point on the stove, "Ready," she said "To chuck ower his f——g heed."

She definitely would have carried out her threat if he had been brainless enough to creep under one of her windows.

Another insight into her character is when one night, one of her sons, Lawrence, came home exceptionally drunk, much too drunk for her liking, and started being very argumentative and aggressive, so she promptly emptied a pot of hot tea over his head. Another night she threw a large carving knife aimed at son Cyril, the only reason being, he had the audacity to answer her back. The knife skimmed past his ear, only missing him by an inch or so, and being flung so vehemently, it wedged about two inches into the wooden door behind him. He shivered and mused, "Was she a bad shot, or had she really meant to miss him?"

Another younger son Horace came home one day bruised and bleeding, the result of having been attacked by another young man after an intense argument. Granny Sarah upon seeing his bloodied face screamed, "Whee did that to yi?"

Horace told her the name of his attacker,

"Where is 'ee now?" she bellowed.

Horace supplied her with details of his whereabouts, and provided with the information, she instantly wiped her floury hands on her pinny. The baking of bread could wait; she had more important issues to deal with, and with that, she stormed out of the house, all four feet ten inches of her.

As she approached Horace's assailant, who was at the time standing in front of a shop window casually smoking a cigarette, she swiftly lurched forward, grabbed him by his lapels, then bodily lifted him up and proceeded to throw him straight through the plate glass window of the shop.

She stood and watched as he delicately pushed himself up and dusted the shards of glass off his clothing. He was trembling like a leaf; unable to comprehend what had just happened. Fortunately, he was not seriously injured, and Granny, somewhat satisfied with herself, shouted "Yi berrer think twice before bullying any of my sons in future."

Granny had a brother named Tom, whose marriage was very tempestuous and volatile. Therefore, on several occasions, after arguments, Tom's wife would leave the marital home, only to return after things had calmed down. Regrettably, Tom died very suddenly after suffering a massive heart attack, and on the day of his funeral, relatives and friends congregated at the cemetery to pay their last respects. Obviously, amongst the mourners was Tom's wife, who being very distraught, was standing at the graveside sobbing and crying. Granny Sarah looked at her in contempt and scornfully shouted, "Warra hypocrite. If yi think so much of 'im, then join im."

With that, she pushed her down into the grave, where she landed on top of Tom's coffin. The other mourners looked on dumbstruck, not daring to make any comments, and it was only when Granny turned to walk away several people rushed forward to help the shocked trembling wife from out of the deep hole.

Every Saturday lunch time. Granny sent her youngest son Cyril (my uncle) to the local fish and chip shop to purchase a hot meal for her large family. Because there would be ten portions, Cyril always asked me to accompany him, to help carry them home.

One particular Saturday, after being served, we made our way home and handed the portions of fish and chips over to Granny who started to unfold the newspapers in which they were wrapped. It was a spectacle to witness her face slowly changing. I watched as her eyes narrowed into slits then a deep frown formed on her brow. Her mouth seemed to shrink into thin lines as she pursed her lips to blow out a slow deliberate breath. She stared at the fish and chips in disbelief; in her opinion, the portions were much too measly. "Reet, cum wi me," she yelled at Cyril and me.

She purposefully dragged us back to the fish shop where she hollered at Cyril, "WHEE SORVED YI?"
Cyril pointed to one of the shop assistants.
"DID YEE SORVE IM THESE?" shouted Granny,
The shop assistant nonchalantly glanced over, and as if she could not give a hoot, replied casually, "Yeh, WHY?" In a contemptuous voice,
Granny was infuriated "I'LL GIVE YI WHY, YI F——G WHORE," she screamed "YI CAN TAAK THESE BACK."

She began to throw the portions of fish and chips, one at a time, at the assistant; her aim was perfect, and each portion found its target, her head. On contact, each packet burst open and the contents rained all over the assistant. She was screaming and covering her face with her hands trying to protect herself from the hot food.
What a mess, the fish and chips were matted in amongst her hair and dropping onto her face and shoulders. They were splattered over her apron, and as expected, the floor ended up a slippery mess being covered with pieces of greasy fish and chips.
"NOW GIVE IS PROPER PORTIONS," Granny

thundered,

Scowling, she stood defiant, hands on hips, legs planted firmly astride; she meant business.

The poor assistant was shaking like a leaf as she began to wrap up another ten portions, which she meekly handed over to Granny.

The other customers in the shop were standing as if rivetted to the spot, shocked at the spectacle they were witnessing. They looked sheepishly away, not wanting to make eye contact with Granny for fear of repercussions.

After Granny had snatched the replacement portions, she said to the assistant "Take a GOOD luk at this lad," pushing the embarrassed Cyril forward,

"And divin't EVER sorve im wi stingy portions EVER again."

With that, she flounced out of the shop.

On the other hand, Granny could be kindness itself. This was demonstrated when one frosty winter's day; a ragged old tramp came begging at her door. She welcomed him with open arms by inviting him in from the cold, and sitting him in a comfortable chair by the roaring fire, to warm himself up. She gave him a large bowl of homemade broth with a couple of hefty chunks of thickly buttered crusty homemade bread and afterwards gave him a couple of shillings, wished him good luck and sent him on his way. I suppose there must have been a grapevine for tramps because several others turned up on her doorstep and all received the same kindness and consideration.

Chapter 8

I went on to win championship titles every year from the age of twelve up until the age of sixteen, which included the Northumberland N.A.B.C. Championship, the Northern Area Championship, and the A.B.A. Championship. I also gained victories against champions from all other areas of the country to reach the national finals.

When I was fourteen, I travelled to Somme Army Barracks in Sheffield, to box in the semi finals of the English championships. This was a featherweight contest and I had trained exceptionally hard but being a growing young man, I was finding it more and more difficult to make the weight. Two weeks before the fight I realised I was five pounds overweight, so had to train in the boiler room of Grainger Park club every night wearing jumpers and coats, which made me sweat profusely. However this did the trick and fortunately I made the weight.

On the day of my fight, Skipper Teasdale hired a bus to take me to Sheffield, which departed from Grainger Park club early in the morning. Aboard were myself, my father, who was to be my corner man, the two club trainers who were Jack Badger and Tommy Caldwell and as many of my faithful supporters the bus could accommodate. We arrived at Sheffield for the scheduled weigh-in, which was lunchtime. Immediately the weigh-in had concluded, father decided there were better things to do than sitting around waiting for the boxing to commence, so he disappeared with Jack and Tommy for a booze up.

Unfortunately, the boxing commenced whilst I was still waiting patiently in the dressing rooms for father to return, and since there wasn't any sign of him, and my own bout was imminent, I had to request another trainer bandage and tape my hands.

It was whilst climbing into the ring, anxious and fearful something might have happened to father, that he suddenly appeared. When I caught sight of him, I was mortified - I felt so humiliated. He was in such a degree of intoxication that he could barely stand up. He dragged himself up the ring steps, fell through the ropes then collapsed comatose onto the canvas at my feet. At that precise moment, I heard someone at the ringside loudly utter "Just look at the state of him; isn't that disgraceful."

Feeling thoroughly ashamed I bent down, pulled him onto to his feet and as I pushed him out through the ropes I growled into his ear, "Get out the ring and sit down you drunken old bastard. How could you show me up like this?"

Understandably, my mind was not on the fight. I had never felt so self-conscious and belittled in all my life, to be disgraced in front of crowds of spectators; I just wished the floor would open and swallow me up.

However even though I was feeling extremely embarrassed, I was winning the fight, but there was something niggling me. I knew something was wrong, but being upset I could not seem to work the problem out.

At the end of the second round, even though he was extremely drunk, father dragged himself to my corner and slurred into my ear "Why aren't yi throwing yer right hand? Can't yi see ee's a southpaw?"

Up until that contest, I had never in my entire career boxed a southpaw, so immediately realised it was his unorthodox style causing the problem. As a result, from the beginning of the third round, I reverted to throwing my right hand and proceeded to knock my opponent all over the ring, finally dumping him onto the canvas to win the fight, which meant I had qualified for the England Championship final at Leeds.

After the fight, I told father in no uncertain terms that

he would never, under any circumstance, accompany me to any of my fights in future. I wanted to make sure there would be absolutely no repeat of the disgraceful humiliation I had been put through.

My next contest was to box in the 'All England Finals,' at Leeds. Since Skipper Teasdale was not able to accompany me, he arranged for Billy Woodruff, who was his second in command to escort me. Billy and I boarded a train at Newcastle Central station to make the journey to Leeds and when the train reached Durham City a female climbed into our carriage and sat opposite us. I glanced at her and noticed she was an exceptionally common looking woman. Her face was plastered with thick orange makeup, with lips painted thickly with shiny bright red lipstick and she was wearing vivid blue eye shadow smeared up to her eyebrows. Her bleached yellow blonde hair had re-growth of dark roots showing through. She must have been in her late forties, and definitely, mutton dressed as lamb.

She started to chat to Billy, making very suggestive remarks, and made several comments with double meanings. She enquired where we were going and Billy replied, "Leeds."
He explained to her that I was boxing in the N.A.B.C. finals. She peered hard at me and to my acute embarrassment, her eyes lowered and focused intensely on my crotch. She said, "I bet he has plenty of lead in his pencil."

I felt embarrassed and self-conscious; and felt my face

slowly turning bright red. As we alighted from the train. Billy informed me she was a prostitute on her way to London to find work.

After the Leeds Championship contest, I was chosen to represent Great Britain, the venue being Wembley. A momentous achievement I felt; I trained harder than ever and was determined to reach my full potential.

There was massive coverage given of my success in the local press, and as most of the local shopkeepers wanted me to succeed. Thinking good food would help to make me stronger, they rallied round and kindly made donations to me. The butcher supplied me with steak, the fish shop donated fish and eggs, and the greengrocer gave me fresh fruit and vegetables. I greatly appreciated this kindness and thanked them wholeheartedly.

Alas, to everyone's great disappointment, a week before the contest I contracted influenza. I desperately tried to fight against the illness and somehow managed to persuade the doctor, against his better judgment, to allow me to fight. However, suffering from the after effects of flu and weakened and impaired by the lack of training, I lost the contest on points.

During that period, I lived for sport, not only for boxing, which of course was my first love, but I also took great pleasure in playing football. I was honoured to be selected to play for Grainger Park football team, and I was also a member of my school team. South Benwell, although I could only play in the school team if I borrowed a pair of football boots. There was a boy in my class called Billy Donaldson who was usually kind enough to lend me his elder brother Billy's boots. Billy, nicknamed Poppy, was actually a professional footballer who played centre forward for Newcastle United, so I was very proud to have the privilege of donning his boots.

Being athletic, I swam strongly and won many competitions for both Grainger Park club and South Benwell School.

It was during 1948 when a delegation of Russian dignitaries visited Great Britain to discover how our country was recovering from the ravages of war. At that time, it was customary for large gangs of youths to either hang about on street corners, or gather in pubs for excessive drinking sessions, so inevitably they would end up drunk and start fighting.

There were frequent stories in all the newspapers, national and local, relating tales of drunken brawls and loutish behaviour of British youths.

I was aged fourteen at the time and lived for sport. Consequently, since I was so dedicated I spent all my spare time at Grainger Park gym, training and entering boxing contests, the thought of gangs and street fighting never entered my mind and had no place in my life.

After their evaluation of our country, the shocked Russian delegation departed from our shores and returned home to Russia, once home, they described the appalling scenes they had witnessed at first hand in Britain, and related all the unsavoury stories, chronicled in the British press, about the atrocious antics of the British Youth. They went on to describe the young men of Britain as indolent, impolite, uncouth and foulmouthed troublemakers; the widespread adverse publicity in Russia was apparently discussed in the House of Lords.

Soon afterwards, Skipper Teasdale summoned me to his office, where two newspaper reporters, who, I was informed, came from Manchester, confronted me then proceeded to interview, and question me for about half an hour. Since I was very successful in the ring at that particular time. I clearly believed they were interested in my boxing career, although rather puzzled by the nature of their questions; the dialogue was completely different from the normal questions, reporters usually asked me. In that, they were specifically probing me about, not only my sporting achievements, but were delving into my personal private life and grilling me about girlfriends, home life and school life.

I informed them I didn't have much time for girls, as I spent all my spare time training at the gym, but if I did have a girlfriend I would respect her, I made it clear I was very happy at home, and I had been promoted to deputy head boy at school.

About a week later, another two reporters came to the gym to interview me, they asked comparable questions, so of course being curious, I asked Skipper Teasdale

"Why all the interest in me?'

He told me that apparently the media throughout Britain had taken umbrage with the objectionable interpretation made about British youth in the Russian Press. Therefore, had orchestrated a plan to choose a youth, who, by example, would be a credit to Britain.

In reality, youth clubs throughout Great Britain were requested to select a youth from within their members, who could, in their opinion, possibly symbolise the role model of 'The Perfect British Youth'.
Unbeknown to myself. Skipper Teasdale, who had always thought highly of me had selected myself and put my name forward as being his choice from Grainger Park Club, hence all the interviews.

A few weeks later, as usual, I arrived at the club for training but this time, as soon as I walked through the door, Skipper Teasdale asked me to go to his office where I found him jubilant and unable to contain his delight. He was beaming from ear to ear and said to the great delight and honour of the club I had been chosen as the role model to symbolise British youth. I was astounded by the news and it took ages to sink in, but I felt very privileged and proud. Skipper Teasdale immediately organised a public ceremony to be held at Grainger Park Club and invited Lord Ravensworth, one of the club's beneficiaries, to present me with a Charter.
The Charter was printed on parchment and set behind glass within a wooden frame and was fashioned in a similar style to the Ten Commandments. There were

'Ten Rules', which I had to swear to adhere to.

The public ceremony was very well attended and the hall was brimming with spectators, including my parents and relatives who were elated with my accomplishment and my proud headmaster who found time from his busy schedule to attend and congratulate me. There were Journalists from several regions, who reported the event in detail giving it coverage in the national newspapers.

Chapter 9

Shortly before my fifteenth birthday and having only a few weeks of schooling left, a boxing referee, Mr Leonard Dressner, who had closely followed my amateur career, approached me, asking if I had any employment lined up for when I finished school. I replied,
"I haven't even thought about an occupation yet."

He explained to me that he had his own floor laying business, and offered me employment, as an apprentice. I was very grateful for the offer, accepted, and began to work on the first Monday after leaving school. This being my first job, I was quite nervous but also eager to do well. My apprenticeship was to learn the trade of laying sand and cement floors, screeding floors and also to lay tiles and linoleum. This training was to last for a period of three years.

It was three weeks after I began working the firm obtained a new contract which was to lay a complete new floor at a large local factory. I had settled in well and was enjoying the work, though being the new apprentice, it was required I ran errands and I was expected to make the tea.

On the first day of working at the factory, at morning break-time I was asked to take our large brown teapot down to the canteen to obtain boiling water. The foreman said he had forgotten to bring a bottle of milk in to work, so told me to, "Ask the canteen supervisor nicely, if she would kindly add milk to the boiling water."

I measured four teaspoons of dried tealeaves into the teapot and made my way downstairs to the canteen. I politely asked the supervisor if she could add some milk but she was very mean and unpleasant and refused point blank. I tried to persuade her by turning on the charm but to no avail; she was adamant, the milk was for canteen workers only and NOT for outside contractors.

After she filled the teapot with boiling water, I picked it up, one hand holding the spout and the other holding the handle, then being very fit and agile I started to leap back up the stairs taking them two at a time.

Regrettably, I tripped on one of the stair treads, as I fell forward, the pot struck the staircase and the entire pot of scalding tea emptied over my head and face. I began to howl out with pain and in a matter of seconds; I was surrounded by numerous office staff, who upon hearing the racket came to my assistance.

One girl ran to telephone for an ambulance and another ran to the first aid cabinet where she grabbed a bottle of calamine lotion and applied it all over my face and neck, which to my relief cooled the burning sensation and soothed the pain slightly. The ambulance arrived within fifteen minutes to whisk me off to Newcastle General Hospital. It was whilst being treated by the doctor that he explained to me, I should consider myself to be very, very lucky, because if there had been milk in the tea I would have been permanently scarred. I was extremely thankful the penny-pinching canteen supervisor had refused my request for the milk.

After treatment, I caught sight of myself in a mirror and I was amused to see I resembled the invisible man. My whole head and neck were completely swathed in bandages, incorporating small openings for my eyes, a tiny hole so that I could breathe through my nose and a small opening for my mouth.

After receiving hospital assistance, the doctor arranged for an ambulance to take me home, but as we neared my house, I realised that mother would have a fit if she observed the ambulance drawing up outside the house, so I requested the driver drop me off at the top of our street. However when I walked into the house, mother almost collapsed with shock "Is that you, our Ronnie?" she whispered.

"Yes mother, but don't worry, I'm o.k." I said

After a few moments, I managed to reassure her that I was fine and I described what had happened and told her the doctor was confident there would be no scarring. She visibly calmed down and appeared to be very relieved.

Unfortunately after working for just eighteen months, the floor laying company found themselves in financial difficulties and subsequently went into voluntary liquidation.

Hence I found myself out of a job. It was at that time, a wealthy young man, who was about two years older than I was, visited Grainger Park gym on several occasions. He was extremely well spoken, having been educated at either Oxford or Cambridge; he always make a beeline to engage me in conversation. He said that he was fascinated with boxing and had followed my career with interest.

Skipper Teasdale informed me the young man was John Fenwick Jnr., son of the owner of Fenwick Ltd, a vast prestigious department store in the centre of Newcastle, which is currently widely accepted as being the 'Harrods of the North.' Fenwick's incidentally were patrons of Grainger Park Boys' club therefore made numerous large monetary donations. Skipper said Mr John Fenwick Snr. upon hearing of my circumstances from son John had created a position for me in his department store, and if I accepted his offer, I could start work the following Monday. I was delighted, given that only two weeks had elapsed since being made redundant from my floor laying apprenticeship, so I felt privileged to be offered a job at such short notice and gratefully accepted.

Monday morning arrived, and being apprehensive I was up with the larks. I dressed in my smartest clothes then went to catch a bus into the city centre. I arrived at Fenwick's and as instructed I reported to a Miss Hall who was a middle-aged woman with grey hair swept into a French chignon. She smelled heavily with the scent of lavender and was particularly well spoken and very courteous to me.

She said a position had been especially created for me. The job was to collect orders for ice cream from the three 'in store' restaurants and the cafe. I then had to make my way to the warehouse and collect the ice cream for delivery. I was also expected to keep a stock check and inform Miss Hall when the ice cream was running low so that she could re-order.

This job took only a very small chunk of time out of an eight-hour working day, so instead of lazing around and feeling bored stiff, I would often help the store porters to unload deliveries from vans into the warehouse, even though it was not part of my duties.

Weather permitting, during our lunch hour, the porters, van drivers and myself would play football in the back lane behind Fenwick's store. It was during one kick-a-bout I booted the ball too high and it sailed up through the air to land onto the roof of the building opposite, which was a YMCA hostel. One of the porters departed, only to appear a moment later carrying a long extension ladder, which he promptly propped up against the wall. Since it was my fault, I was responsible for retrieving the ball; therefore, I climbed carefully up the ladder and stepped onto the roof. I looked around and observed the ball lying near the edge of the roof, which was about twenty feet away. As I walked across the roof to retrieve it, I suddenly found myself crashing through a glass roof light, which was so weathered and dirty I had not noticed it.

Thankfully my reflexes were so finely tuned that as I plummeted through, I managed to grab an iron bar, positioned across the window. As I was undulating and hanging on for dear life, I glanced below and saw I was precariously suspended about thirty feet above ground level. I noticed there were rows of cast iron bedsteads positioned in a line on the concrete floor beneath me. My heart was pounding, knowing if I fell I could die; I used all my strength to cautiously drag myself back up through the broken window. However as I was clambering out onto the roof, I felt the sharp pain of a jagged piece of glass cutting deeply across my forearm, which consequently started pouring with blood. As I descended the ladder, the other employees saw the blood running down my arm and dripping off my fingers and rushed forward to give assistance, then called an ambulance.

The wound was a large V shaped cut with the narrow end of skin tucked firmly inside. Once at the hospital I didn't have to wait long before a nurse attended to me. She began to use a metal hook-like instrument with which she poked around, trying to pull the skin back out from the wound. Because it was exceptionally painful, I was flinching with pain and the nurse said in an exasperated voice, "Don't be such a baby; you'll never be a soldier."

I was so angry I retorted, "I don't want to be a f——g soldier."

The nurse finished cleaning and stitching the wound, and realising I might have offended her by using bad language I apologised to her.

She replied, "Don't worry I would have said exactly the same; anyway that's nothing to what we have to put up with when all the drunks come in on a Saturday night. Your language was tame; we hear all the swear words and oaths you could ever imagine and more, plus we often have to endure physical violence."

It was shortly afterwards, the lads at Fenwick's suggested I arrange a friendly football match between our employees at Fenwick's and the Grainger Park Club team, I was happy to oblige and enjoyed organising the match, which was held on an extremely cold Saturday afternoon in winter. The ground was rock hard with frost, but being a friendly game it was allowed to commence. However Grainger Park found they were a player short, since one of the lads in their team had taken ill.

My father had unexpectedly arrived to watch the match, so I approached him and cajoled and pressurised him until he finally agreed to play for them, even though he was unfit and in his forties.

During the whole duration of the match, the Fenwick's player who was marking father, and who incidentally was an ex heavyweight professional boxer and twice the size of father, pushed and shoved him all over the pitch. However, father, having great determination, stayed on for the whole ninety minutes.

I watched in amusement as father worked hard throughout the whole of the match running himself to exhaustion. Consequently next day, he could hardly move; he was so stiff he was almost rigid and his whole body ached with pain. As he lay in bed moaning, he whispered, "I can't move a muscle; the only parts of my body I can move are my eyes. I can't go to the pub, and I'll be in bed for weeks."

It was only then that I realised he was actually feeling ill, as this was the one and only time I can ever remember him missing the pub on a Sunday morning.

Chapter 10

As an amateur boxer, I was earning quite a reputation in the area; therefore, I was finding it increasingly difficult to get contests. Frequently, I arrived at a venue, strong, fit, and looking forward to the match, only to find my opponent had cried off. This was soul destroying, after all my hard work and dedicated training over the weeks, I would be very frustrated and I became so exasperated I decided, even though I was only sixteen, to turn professional. I rang Joe Shepherd who was the local professional boxing promoter/matchmaker and explained my predicament. Since he was always scouting for talent, he immediately recognised me, and said that he had been following my amateur career very closely and would be very interested to meet me to discuss my future. He invited me for an assessment, to his professional boxing gym at the Savoy, which was an obsolete dance hall situated on Armstrong Road. This was very conveniently located for me, it being only about one mile from home. Joe arranged for me to box a few rounds with a Jimmy Muirhead, who was a local welterweight professional fighter, so he could determine my abilities.

After observing me boxing several rounds, he said he was very impressed and told me in his opinion I should go far in the fight game. He advised me not to bother with a manager, saying he could arrange all my fights. He arranged for officials from the British Boxing Board of Control to observe me boxing at his gym in order to obtain my licence. He also sorted out the required medical examination and I passed both with flying colours. My professional licence was duly processed.
I was raring to go but Joe said: "Because you are only sixteen, there is no urgency. Bide your time; wait until I promote an important European Title bill and I will arrange your debut bout on that."

Soon afterwards, following intense training, Joe arranged my first professional fight and my employers, Fenwick's were incredibly helpful and considerate as they allowed me two weeks off work, as paid holiday, meaning I could train full time to achieve supreme fitness. They also displayed a large photograph of me in boxing pose in the huge display window of their store in Northumberland Street, Newcastle upon Tyne. Phil

Fowler, who was an older porter at Fenwick's, and was an ex professional boxer himself, helped me tremendously with my training. Phil had sustained an injury serving in the Second World War, which had blinded him in one eye, and it seems he had boxed all his professional fights, unbeknown to the boxing authorities, with sight in one eye only.

My professional fight debut was as a lightweight; at New St. James's Hall, Newcastle upon Tyne. This was, as Joe Shepherd had promised, on the European Flyweight championship bill, which featured top of the bill, Teddy Gardiner of West Hartlepool v Louis Skeena of France, over fifteen rounds for the title.

Joe matched me against Teddy Gardiner's chief sparring partner, John Marshall who was an experienced boxer from West Hartlepool. This being my debut appearance, it was scheduled over four rounds.

Unfortunately this first fight I lost on points, although the next morning upon purchasing The Newcastle Journal which is a local newspaper, I was delighted to read the report of the fight in the sports column, which stated:-

'Jackson lost on points, but the only man in the hall who thought Marshall had won was the referee. Everyone else thought Jackson had won hands down'

Reading this article give me a great boost.

My next fight was against John Dyers: -I won on points.

My next bout was against Bill Fryers: - This one I also won on points.

The next bout was against Jeff Walters: -I lost this one when I sustained a badly cut eye, which needed six stitches.
The next contest was against Tommy Mount: -I won on points.

New St. James' Hall was a famous venue for boxing shows in the North East and was nicknamed the Graveyard of Champions. It was renowned as having the most derogatory and demonstrative of any audience throughout the country since the Newcastle spectators were always highly critical and very hard to please. Whilst they appreciated good boxing, the wisecracks would come thick and fast and everyone assumed that if you could please the Newcastle crowd, you could confidently box anywhere else in the country.

One night after one of my fights, I joined the rest of the spectators to watch the bill; the subsequent fight was a scheduled eight rounds welterweight contest. As the boxers climbed through the ropes into the ring, the audience noticed one of them was wearing high-legged white American style leather boots, with long laces, which hung almost like tassels to virtually touch the floor, the like of which had never been seen before in the Newcastle hall. The crowd's reaction was, as expected, hilariously funny, when out of the blue a loud voice quipped up from the top gallery: -
"Oh you hop a little on your little left shoe."
There came riotous laughter and applause from the

Professional, at Sixteen.

spectators, then a quiet pause, then suddenly a voice from the opposite side of the hall: -

"You hop a little on your right one too."

This banter continued throughout the whole contest, but to give credit to both boxers, it was a tremendous fight, and well appreciated by the audience.

If the criticising viewers were disappointed with a boxers' performance, the witticisms would come thick and fast: such as: -

"Wore lass cud beat these two, wi one hand tied behind er back."

Yet another spectator would bellow loud and clear, "Handbags at five paces."

It was on such a bill at St. James's Hall, that a top class American heavyweight clambered through the ropes into the ring. However, being a late substitute, he was unfit and at least two stones over his normal fighting weight, and regrettably he did not know what he was letting himself in for. After he removed his dressing gown in his corner, exposing rolls of excess fat, the Mickey-takers went into top gear and the one-liners came in quick customary fashion.

"When's it due?"

"How far gan are yi pet?"

"Eee divin't drop it in the ring."

"Can I taak yi haem, wore kid needs a new bouncy baal."

"Eee it's Mr Michelin Man."

He must have been one of the countless boxers relieved to climb out of the ring to escape the derogatory remarks.

It was two days after my birthday, on the 12th August 1952 when having reached the age of eighteen, the dreaded envelope dropped through our letterbox from Her Majesty's Service, instructing me to enrol for the obligatory two years National Service into the army, to serve my Queen and Country. Upon arriving at the recruitment office, I was full of trepidation as I sat down to fill in the mandatory forms. Subsequently, after passing the medical I was persuaded to sign on for an extra year, having being swayed by the fact the income paid in the regular army was about three times higher than it was for National Servicemen, and also the reality I would be able to learn a trade was another major motive in my decision.

It was after all the legalities had been concluded I was consequently drafted into the Royal Electrical Mechanical Engineers, the R.E.M.E, and a few days later, having been supplied with travelling instructions and a rail pass, I boarded a train at Newcastle Central Station to travel by train to my destination, Dorset. I was quite excited not knowing what was in store for me, and sensed this was the beginning of a new chapter in my life.

Now that is another story.

Chapter 11

It was July 1955 when I arrived back in Newcastle, on
two weeks demobilisation leave. I felt very weird, having
being away from home for three years. The area felt
unfamiliar and strange as I strolled out of Newcastle
Central Station to join a queue waiting for a bus, which
would take me home. I arrived at my parents' house
thirty minutes later to be confronted with a tremendous
welcome from my family who had organised a surprise
coming home party and although I am not the partying
type, it was great to be home. I could hardly recognise
my younger sisters, Jeanne and Lilian as they had grown
so much.

That first night home, I went with father to the

Hydraulic pub on Scotswood Road for a celebratory drink. There happened to be a stranger standing at the bar with a drink in his hand, who was bragging about his army experiences and reeling off all the countries he had supposedly served in, and was describing all the actions which he had been involved in during the war.

At first, most of the regular drinkers were predominantly intrigued when listening to his stories, but since he went on and on, bragging and boasting, soon everyone became thoroughly bored. They assumed he must be romancing, and believed the stories must be fictitious, considering the tales that were unfolding were so outrageous.

Undeterred, he puffed out his chest and proudly alleged: "I have a medal with a bar."
Father having a very dry wit, casually piped up: "I have three bars."
The stranger's jaw dropped: "THREE?" he said in disbelief.
My father nonchalantly quipped: "Yes, three - The Hydraulic, The Hammer and The Gun."

These being three of the most popular bars on Scotswood Road, everyone in the pub burst out laughing, and with that the stranger drank up his beer and left.

After the initial pleasure of coming home, I soon began to feel despondent and at a loose end, since all my pre army mates were now either in the army themselves, or courting, so, having been accustomed to the constant companionship of close mates over the past three years, I was feeling incredibly lonely. A few nights later, thoroughly bored, I decided to make my way to the Oxford Galleries, which was a popular dance hall in the centre of Newcastle.

The Oxford was a famous popular meeting place for young couples, and it was widely accepted, more than fifty per cent of the local population met their future spouses there.

I was generally milling amongst the crowds of young people, whilst listening to the live music playing at full blast from the raised stage. I watched as couples danced together on the highly polished floor whilst the compulsory revolving bulbous glass hanging lights created diamonds of lights, which flickered across the room. Suddenly my eyes were drawn like a magnet to a girl, the most stunning girl I had ever seen. It was her eyes that first captivated me; big, dark brown Latin type eyes. When she looked at me, and our eyes met, I felt my heart begin to race. It may sound corny, but it was love at first sight. Even though she was small in stature, being only five feet two inches tall, she had an aura of elegance about her; she was slim with a trim petite figure.

She was wearing a pale apple green blouse, which was tucked into a dark charcoal grey pencil skirt and wore high stiletto heels which added another four inches to her height. Her dark brunette hair was cut short with two little kiss curls brought onto her forehead, this being the modern style at that time.

I decided to make my way over to ask her to dance and pushed my way through the crowds of young couples, only to be disappointed when reaching the spot, to discover some other guy had beaten me to it. I was determined to introduce myself so lingered at the edge of the dance floor waiting until the music stopped. As she walked by, I took her hand, introduced myself, and asked for the next dance.

As we danced to the music, we chatted happily and I discovered she was seventeen years old, her name was Wyn, and she worked in a solicitors' office. Coincidently she lived very near to my home, in fact, on the private housing estate, which was at the top of my street. When the music ended and we were making our way off the dance floor, we somehow became separated by the huge crowd of dancers bustling past us. I frantically searched and searched, looking though the hordes of people, but was distraught when I was unable to find her, and I went home extremely disillusioned.

I couldn't get Wyn out of my mind, and several times, every single day for the next ten days of my demob leave, I walked through the estate Wyn lived on, hoping I would bump into her, but to my frustration and disappointment I never did.

All too soon, the day came when I had to return to Aldershot to be demobbed and during the train journey south, I couldn't stop thinking about the girl I had met with the most wonderful eyes. During the next two weeks I could not concentrate, and couldn't wait to return to Newcastle to try to find her again.

That day finally arrived, and upon returning to Newcastle after being demobbed, I again, with optimism, resumed my daily walks through the housing estate on which Wyn lived but to no avail. I was obsessed with finding her, and was beginning to despair, thinking that day would never come.

I was again alone and at a loose end, when one night, strolling along the West Road in Newcastle, I unexpectedly bumped into an old school mate who said he had a free ticket for the Brighton dance hall, which was only about twenty yards away.
He said he was not going to use it, as he had a date, so he offered me the ticket. I was in two minds whether to accept, but then, I think it must have been intuition, I seemed to have a strong premonition I should accept - maybe I'd inherited my father's psychic powers.

As soon as I walked into the dance hall, I could not believe my eyes- there she was, the girl of my dreams. This time she was wearing a dark bottle green satin sleeveless dress nipped in at the waist; the skirt was full, this being the high fashion in the fifties. My stomach turned cartwheels. I immediately made a made a beeline for her, and as I approached, she recognised me and smiled, this time I held her hand persistently, to make sure that I would never lose her again. Wyn told me she had seen me searching among the crowds that night at the Oxford and was hoping I was looking for her. Taking her on to the dance floor, I enveloped her in my arms, pulling her close to me as we danced to the music, I nestled my face into her hair, which had a lovely light fragrant scent. Every so often, I would push her gently away so I could gaze into her big brown eyes and kiss her. I could not believe the way I felt, me the tough, supremely fit athlete reduced to this weak-kneed trembling wreck.

"So this is love!"

In the past, I had had many girlfriends; however I had never felt this way before, so I knew instantly I wanted to spend the rest of my life with her. I told Wyn I loved her; she replied she felt the same, and it had been love at first sight for her also. That was the beginning of our life together. Wyn was quite shy and incredibly modest. I persistently flattered her and would tell her how gorgeous she was, but she used to laugh and say that I saw her through rose-coloured spectacles. She was my destiny, my soul mate, my best friend.

I loved her so much I could not bear to let her out of my sight so we met every single day until eventually, six months later, we took the ultimate commitment of marriage.

The wedding took place at our local church, St. James's, bringing back memories of my childhood escapade.

Wyn.

Brother Stan was my best man and Wyn's sister Joyce and my sister Jeanne were bridesmaids, Jeanne was elated - never before had she owned such a beautiful new dress. It was pale blue in colour and was made from satin and lace. Jeanne felt like a princess as she proudly twirled in front of the mirror.

During the wedding ceremony I felt very proud as I stood next to my wife at the altar. I was ecstatic and my life seemed complete. I jokingly said I had been half way around the world, and then met, fell in love with and married a girl from the top of my street.

Chapter 12

Finding myself back in Civvy Street, after completing my army service, I was undecided upon which occupation to pursue. Since I had been quite frugal in the army, I had saved several hundred pounds so I reached the decision, I should become self-employed. In that era, most of the properties in the neighbourhood had open fires on which they burned coal and logs, so I decided it could be quite a good little money earner if I bought and sold logs to housewives around the local streets.

I scrutinised through the advertisements in the 'Commercial vehicles for sale' column in the local newspaper and noticed a Hillman van which I thought would be suitable. It was described as being reliable and clean, and was only £45. It sounded ideal for my requirements, so I arranged to inspect and check it over. On initial examination, the van seemed to be in good nick, so I purchased it there and then. However at that time there were no such restrictions as M.O.T's. Now, in hindsight, I am convinced if there had been such checks, the van would never have passed, not in a million years. It would have failed miserably, and I believe it would surely have been consigned to the scrap heap.

I normally parked the van overnight in the back lane, outside my parents' house, which was on an incredibly precipitous hill and each day I requested father accompany me, primarily for companionship and the other reason being, to keep him out of the boozer for a few hours. Every morning I drove to a nearby local colliery to purchase logs, which were old pit props that had already been sawn up by the miners, into the correct size. We arrived at the pit to load the logs into the van, cramming them in as tightly as possible, and on the way home, stopped in each of the streets that we drove through, to sell the logs to the residents. The van was invariably empty by the time we reached home, since this being an economical way to produce heat, the logs were extremely popular and in great demand.

It was during this winter that we were experiencing an unusually sub-zero spell, so on an especially bitterly cold morning, the temperature being several degrees below freezing, when I tried to start the van it was unresponsive. After numerous attempts and still getting no reaction, (being a clapped-out wreck this was nothing unusual), I began to feel anxious, thinking the battery was becoming flat, so I said to father. "Get in; I'll try to bump start it down the hill."

I disengaged the handbrake and began to freewheel the vehicle down the steep bank. I tried letting the clutch out several times but the van was as dead as a doornail. I was becoming rather desperate as I was nearing the road junction at Scotswood Road. I therefore made one last frantic attempt and finally to my relief, the engine burst into life. I assumed if I took my foot off the accelerator to brake at the junction, the engine would, in all probability, cut out, and almost certainly would not start again. I kept my fingers crossed, hoping the road would be clear of any morning commuter traffic which could be approaching and wrenched the steering wheel round to the right, then recklessly careered onto Scotswood Road.

At that precise moment, as the van hurtled around the corner leaning over, almost on two wheels, without warning, the passenger door flew open and the passenger seat with father still perched on it, shot out of the van and landed slap bang in the middle of the road, father still sitting as if entrenched into it.
I quickly glanced into the mirror and saw father, still perched, bolt upright and motionless on the van seat. He appeared to be frozen with fear, not moving an inch and seemed as if in a trance, the knuckles of his hands white,

as he clutched onto the sides of the seat, hanging on it seemed, for dear life, as the passing traffic swerved left and right to avoid him. Appreciating father hadn't come to any real grief, apart from his dignity and maybe his arse being bruised, I made the split decision to stay in the van to keep the engine running, firmly believing, if I took my foot off the accelerator to go to his aid, the engine would more than likely cut out.

I could not help laughing at the hilarious spectacle he made; I leaned out of my door and shouted. "COME ON FATHER, YOU CAN'T SIT ON YOUR LAZY ARSE ALL DAY, WE'VE GOT WORK TO DO, GET BACK IN."

He stood up and shouted "AAD JUST AS SOON HOY MEESELL OFF THE TYNE BRIDGE AS GET BACK INTO THAT F——G WRECK. IT'S A HEAP OF CRAP"

With that, he picked up the seat, brought it over to the van, opened the back doors, threw it in, slammed the door and stormed off.

During the few weeks prior to being demobbed, I had suffered bouts of severe stomach pain, and since this was persistent, the military doctor advised me, upon arriving home, to seek medical advice from my own civilian doctor. I carried out his advice and after consultation, followed by examination; I was given a prescription for tablets and medicine, with instructions to take both three times daily before and after food. I continued this treatment for several months, but in spite of this, the problem persisted and I was still suffering from unrelenting pain.

After Wyn and I wed, I was having frequent spasms of pain, bouts of sickness and then began to vomit blood. Because of this, my local doctor referred me to a specialist at the Newcastle General Hospital for tests, which involved having a barium meal and stomach X-rays. Unfortunately, the analysis disclosed I had a duodenal ulcer, which to my distress meant I would not be able to resume my professional boxing career until cured. The hospital instructed me to go on a strict dietary routine, and gave me a diet sheet of do's and don'ts. I also purchased a book which I had seen advertised in a local newspaper. "How I Cured My Duodenal Ulcer."

The author recommended eating steamed fish, creamed mashed potatoes and peas, this to be followed by milky rice pudding. The meal had to be consumed every day for six months. Even though it was particularly bland and monotonous Wyn made sure I adhered to it. She would dutifully cook the meal every single day. I ate the boring food religiously day in, day out, and devoutly stuck to the diet, until finally, after many months, the ulcer seemed to have disappeared, and X-ray confirmed this.

At long last, I was pain free, but I was to be disappointed when my own family doctor advised me that I would not pass the medical to renew my boxing licence until a symptom-free year had passed.

It was during these months, and after the van had finally disintegrated and took its place of honour at the top of a scrap heap, that I applied for and was successful in obtaining an apprenticeship. This was to learn a new trade as a food machinery mechanic, meaning after three years I would be a qualified engineer. Unfortunately being an apprenticeship meant the salary was very meagre, therefore paying rent and other bills and having enough money for the usual day-to-day expenses was extremely difficult and it was hard for us to manage.

This is where Wyn's mum, Polly, the best mother-in-law anyone could ever have, came in. She was truly a gem, so kind and generous. Polly was supportive and helped us financially in every way. She bought our food when we were skint, she helped us furnish the flat, which Wyn and I rented, she bought all the decorating materials and then helped to paint and wallpaper throughout. We are beyond doubt forever grateful to her - she is truly a treasure. Wyn has three sisters, an elder sister Joyce, and two younger sisters, Marianne and Carole. Polly's four daughters are her life. She is a typical mother hen, at all times protective, constantly there for them, helping and guiding them every step of the way - woe betide any one who harms one of her beloved daughters.

I can describe Wyn's dad, Ben, as a gentle giant; being six foot two and fourteen stone in weight, he would proudly brag to all and sundry that he had the five best-looking girls in the world. Ben worked as a fitter and

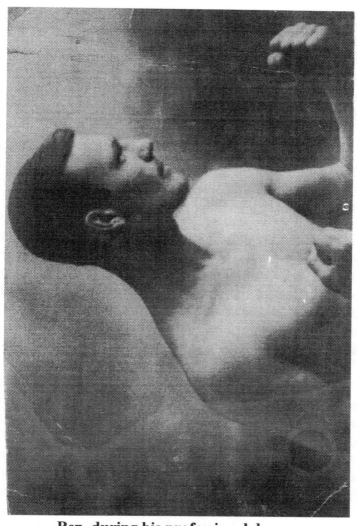

Ben, during his professional days.

turner at Vickers Armstrong's factory on Scotswood Road, and on retirement, after working there for forty years, he received a gold watch, which to me seemed a very paltry pay off, in comparison with modern times' retirement payoffs, which usually consist of tens of thousands of pounds.

Ben was an honest, upstanding family man, being quiet and unassuming, even though he himself had been a professional boxer in his younger years. He was very modest and rarely spoke of his boxing career, but I believe he boxed under the pseudonym of Jack Williams, having had seventeen professional fights knocking sixteen opponents out. Regrettably, as boxing gloves were much inferior to the modern day gloves and because Ben hit so incredibly hard, meant he repeatedly broke his knuckles and therefore had to retire. We became good friends and I always hoped he regarded me as the son he never had.

Ben's father, called Thomas, was also famous in his own right as a professional world sprint champion, winning the one hundred pounds Christmas Handicap at the old Victoria running grounds in Newcastle in 1892. As reigning champion, he threw out a challenge, offering any opponent a ten yards start, promising to give one hundred pounds, to anyone who could beat him. However, I believe he remained unbeaten until he finally retired. He was also a proficient boxer, and won the National Coal Board British boxing Middleweight

Championship, so being a famous sporting celebrity in the area, he had the honour of being chosen to be the starter of the very last Blaydon Races in 1916.

Chapter 13

On the 12th November 1956, Wyn went into labour with our first baby. She began having pains during the night, but typically did not wake me until five thirty in the morning. Wyn had attended the anti natal clinic at Newcastle General Hospital just two days previously, when upon examination, they assured her that, because her 'bump' was so tiny, the baby she was carrying could not possibly be any more developed than 36 weeks, even if that, so she shouldn't expect the baby for at least another month. Because of this information, Wyn assumed the pains must be a false alarm. However as the pains persisted and became more severe we packed her bag and I drove her to Newcastle General Hospital, calling for Polly on the way to accompany us. The hospital confirmed Wyn was in fact, in labour. She was extremely nervous, being only 19 and very nai've, since in those days sex and pregnancy was never openly discussed and sex education was not in the school curriculum.

Looking back, it all seems very antiquated, since relatives were not even allowed to stay with the mother to be, during labour, let alone be present at the birth. Polly and I had to leave Wyn in the delivery room, looking like a frightened little girl. I felt so very guilty.

I hurried to work and explained to my boss, who incidentally had been a sergeant in the R.E.M.E, I needed the day off, explaining Wyn had gone into labour and I felt it was my duty to be at the hospital. He was very understanding but said unfortunately he had just received a telephone call about an urgent repair job, and it was imperative it was attended to before lunch. He apologised saying that, regrettably there was no one else he could send, but he promised I could leave work as soon as I had completed the job. My mind was miles away as I drove to the job which was in Darlington. As I worked on the faulty machine, I just seemed to go through the motions and when I eventually completed the work, I threw my bag of tools into the van, jumped in and quickly headed home.

Arriving at a set of traffic lights, which were on amber, I thought to myself, "I can make it through before they change"

However, I noticed they turned red, as I was halfway across.

My mind being elsewhere, I unfortunately had not noticed the police car behind me. The driver, a police officer in uniform, who of course had witnessed my actions, followed me through the lights, pulled up alongside and signalled me to stop. He parked in front of my van, got out of his car and strolled back to me. I opened my window as he bent down, face level with mine, and asked, "Are you colour blind?"

"No officer." I replied,

Pointing to the traffic lights, he asked, "Which colour comes after yellow?"

"Red, officer." I said.

"Yes! So what does red mean?" he asked.

"Stop." I replied.

"Then why the hell didn't you?" he shouted.

I replied "But officer the lights changed to yellow just as I began to drive through."

I went on to explain my wife was in hospital giving birth to our first baby and I was anxious to get back to Newcastle.

He looked at me in disbelief and said "Pull the other one; I've heard that one before."

I swore it was true. He looked at me wryly, and noticing my anxious face, I suppose he must have believed me, because he smiled, ordered me to reverse back behind the traffic lights. Standing next to my van, he waited until they changed to green, bent down and sarcastically asked, "What colour is that?"

"Green." I replied.

He asked scornfully "What does green mean?"

I said, "It means go officer."

He grinned, said "Go on then, baby won't wait forever."

Gratefully I put my foot down on the accelerator hoping there weren't any more cops in the region and sped back to Newcastle.

I was flustered and anxious when I reached the hospital at 11.45 a.m. only to discover Wyn had just given birth to a little girl. When I saw the tiny bundle, her petite face peeping out of the blankets, eyes blinking against the light I felt a wave of pride surge through me. She was such a beautiful baby so small, so perfect, I felt overwhelmed with happiness. I hugged and kissed Wyn who was crying with emotion. We decided to name the baby Yvonne. She had been born at 11.30 a.m. weighing 6 lb 4 oz.

Yvonne was an extremely good baby and so easy to look after, it was a joy to have this new member in my family. I grabbed every opportunity to take my daughter out for walks, pushing her pram and proudly flaunting her to all and sundry, I was the typical doting dad, and felt this was the beginning of a new chapter in my life.

I soon realised having the extra responsibility of a baby to care for, and not earning a decent wage, meant that things would have to change so I decided my next initiative would be to purchase a van and start my own business as a travelling greengrocer's shop.

In addition, since my ulcer had disappeared, I decided to apply to have my professional licence reinstated, and took the mandatory medical examination, which I passed with flying colours thus obtaining the longed for boxing licence. Being self-employed would mean I could arrange my boxing training around my work and could take time off whenever necessary to follow my boxing career.

I purchased a van by bidding for it in a commercial vehicle auction. It was a three-ton, three-way loader for which I paid £60. I drove the van home full of aspirations and hope. My father arranged for me to meet an acquaintance of his called Alfie Potts, at the greengrocer's wholesale market very early the next Monday morning. Alfie was a very successful businessman, having been in the greengrocery business for numerous years. Previously he had owned twelve fruit and vegetable shops, but was now semi retired. My father had been a casual employee of Alfie's, and had occasionally helped out if he was very busy and short of regular staff.

Monday morning I arrived at the Green Market at six thirty a.m. and met Alfie who instructed me to, "Just keep quiet, stay close to me and watch and learn."

He was beyond doubt a master at haggling and negotiating. He knew all the tricks of the trade, so I learned a great deal from him for which I was eternally grateful.

I believed buying the van as a travelling fruit and vegetable shop was the best venture I could undertake, and arranged to have the lettering: - Ron Jackson, Fruit and Vegetables painted on both sides of the van.

I began what was to become a very lucrative business. I created a worthwhile round with regular customers who relied on me to supply them with fruit and vegetables, so I was soon earning a good living. My regulars appreciated having fresh produce delivered to their door, which alleviated the problem of carrying heavy bags.

Chapter 14

Now it was down to business, serious training for my first comeback professional fight. Each morning I folded my training gear and tucked it behind the driver's seat of my van before setting off for work. Immediately after completing my fruit and vegetable round, I drove to Newcastle Town Moor, usually arriving either early or mid afternoon, and once there, I would run the distance of approximately six miles around the perimeter, whilst simultaneously performing shadow boxing and exercises.

My routine was that each evening after dinner, which we usually ate at 5.30.p.m; I would relax by watching television for a short while, before once more changing into training gear, to drive to the gym, arriving at 7 o'clock. There I would join in with the other boxers to skip, spar, use the punch bag, do masses of exercises, and train until, with the perspiration dripping off me I was practically exhausted. Wyn's dad, Ben, applied to the Boxing Board of Control for a second's licence so he could assist me as my corner man. Ben was perpetually nervous for me, so much so, his hands would tremble when he was bandaging and taping my hands in the dressing rooms. I would mischievously say to him, "It's me fighting Ben, not you; calm down!"

However, no matter how much I tried to reassure him, he always shook like a leaf, but despite his nerves, he was an exceptionally good corner man.

My first comeback fight, which was in fact my sixth professional fight, was duly arranged. I was matched to box Dick Knox of Glasgow in a six rounds welterweight contest at a packed New St. James Hall Newcastle on the 17th February 1958.

Being a tad ring rusty I didn't start well, being out of distance for most of the first round, but to my delight I won by a knockout in the second round.

The Write up next day in our local newspaper by the sports columnist read: -

"Ron Jackson Newcastle (10-4-4) appeared to be nicely started on the way to a points defeat over six rounds against Dick Knox, Glasgow (10-1-3) when suddenly wham: a left hook sent Knox down. Unwisely he got up,

but stood gaping, hands hanging at his sides, as Jackson stepped in and downed him again.

"Too soon he rose again and after a very brief flurry, Jackson nailed him a third time, which was enough for the referee who stopped it there and then though the timekeeper went on counting until he reached 'ten' and it was only the second round."

After this win, I thought I had earned a break from training so rewarded myself with a week of complete rest, before throwing myself back into my usual routine. My next bout was a six round contest against welterweight Brian Husband from Hull. This took place on March 10th 1958 at New St. James' Hall in front of another usual jam-packed audience. I won this contest when Husband sustained a badly cut eye and the referee stopped the fight.

Local sports writer's quote:
" Ron Jackson (Newcastle) boxed very well against a stronger, heavier punching rival in Brian Husband but was probably behind on points when Husband was stopped with a very badly cut eye in the fifth."

My next fight I won, out-pointing Tommy Cavan of Glasgow. Quote by local sports writer:
"Ron Jackson (10-7) came from so far behind to outpoint Tommy Cavan, (10-8-8) over six rounds that he must be rated lucky to win. For sheer guts, his performance had rarely been equalled.

By the fourth, he was bleeding, battered, ready to be knocked out any moment, while Cavan looked strong and fresh, and fully capable. By the middle of the round Jackson was hammering Cavan with lefts and rights and by the finish the Scot was shedding blood and thankful to be still on his feet at the final bell."

In hindsight, I appreciate I should have had a manager and a trainer during my boxing career. If I had been astute enough to employ someone to put my best interests first, my opponents would have been selected more sensibly. I would not have found myself in the predicament of being thrown into contests against boxers who were much more experienced than I was. In addition, the following scenario before my next bout would never have been allowed to happen.

This fight was at a venue in Carlisle, on June 4th 1958. My opponent was the local welterweight Tex Williams, and it was a six three-minute rounds contest. I was enthusiastically looking forward to the bout and after deliberation I decided the best course of action would probably be for me to drive to the location, which was a distance of about 60 or 70 miles. I decided to hire a vehicle, so arranged to collect a hire car at eight o'clock on the morning of the fight, which meant we could take advantage of having the luxury of a brand new car to enjoy. Wyn prepared a packed lunch and made a flask of coffee. We collected a blanket, folded Yvonne's pushchair, and the three of us set off to the seaside. We spent several hours enjoying ourselves on the beach, playing with a ball and splashing about in the water, then early afternoon we drove home and parked the car outside our house and I rested for about an hour.

Wyn cooked a quick snack, then we realised it was time to drop Yvonne off at Polly's as she was babysitting. We hurried out the house and locked the door behind us, only to notice, to our dismay, that the car had a puncture; one of the back tyres was as flat as a pancake. I opened the boot to locate the spare tyre but found, to my frustration, the jack was missing, and as we did not have the luxury of a telephone in those days, we were regrettably unable to request help. I realised there was only one thing for it. I propped the spare wheel against the car, rolled up my sleeves, bent down, and with a spanner, loosened, and took off the wheel nuts. Then standing with my back against the car, I seized the rear end and bodily lifted it up, and with all my strength, held it up in mid air whilst Wyn struggled to take the flat wheel off, after which she had to manoeuvre the spare wheel until she had lined the nut bolts into position, which took quite a while. Nevertheless, she eventually managed, although my strength was sapping with the effort of holding the car up, for what seemed like hours.

After I tightened the nuts onto the spare wheel, we dropped Yvonne off and collected Ben, then I being the only one who could drive, had to face driving the journey of seventy miles. Williams had me down for a count of six in the third round, but I came back strongly and had him down for a count of eight in the last round. He was in trouble but hung on until the final bell, and even though I felt weak as a kitten, I won the fight on points.

On the subject of lifting cars, it reminds me of the night I boxed at a venue in Glasgow, the Kelvin Hall to be precise, when several of my supporters and friends had arrived after driving up from Newcastle to support me. After the bill they made their way back to their cars, where one car load of my fans were truly annoyed to find a Mini was double parked, thus blocking their car in, meaning it was impossible for them to move. They waited for a while chatting and discussing the fights on the bill, then soon became impatient since there was no sign of the Mini's driver and they were anxious to set off for home. They looked at each other and one of them said. "Are you all thinking what I'm thinking?"
They shouted in unison, "Let's do it."

The five physically lifted the Mini, carried it along the road and around a corner, into the next street then set it down in the middle of the road. I can only imagine the face of the driver when he returned to find it had disappeared into thin air. We laughed, as we visualised him frantically searching for it; with a bit of luck he found it quickly.

I won my next bout, against Billy Taylor, on points; however, the following contest, which was against Tony Smith, I lost on points.

I was matched four times against Jimmy Lawson, a welterweight from Middlesbrough. Unfortunately the first of our bouts was stopped when I sustained a very badly cut eye, which required nine stitches. The second of our contests ended in a draw, then the third contest I won on points. However when the fourth contest was arranged, I decided I had to resolve the matter once and for all and I knocked him out in the second round.

Quote by local sports writer:
"Ron Jackson, the Newcastle welterweight, settled his feud with Jimmy Lawson Middlesbrough by knocking his man out in the second round with a combination of left and rights to the chin."

George Cottle from Bermondsey was the opponent for my next bout, but this fight should never have taken place and would definitely have been cancelled if I'd had a manager, as ten days before the fight I was injured. This occurred when a massive iron weight dropped onto my foot, tearing my big toe nail clean out. This wound was excruciatingly painful, and I could hardly walk, let alone execute the required roadwork and skipping in preparation for the fight, so apart from being in acute pain I was unfit.

Quote by local sports writer:
"Jackson was game enough and once in the fourth round, he slammed in a right that caused Cottle's knees to buckle but he was well out pointed. Maybe he would have done better with some of that surplus poundage off."

I was understandably unfit and slightly overweight but this was due to lack of training due to my injury.

My next bout was against Ken Chadwick (Manchester) at New St. James' Hall. This opponent had Wyn particularly worried; she had pre-fight nerves about me fighting Chadwick, as his reputation for being a knockout specialist had preceded him, having stopped his previous five opponents inside the distance. However, Wyn was soon reassured as I won the fight speedily, by stopping him in the second round.

Quote Local Sports writer:
"Ron Jackson made short work of Ken Chadwick. I think Jackson should be stepped up to the eight-round class after stopping Ken Chadwick in the second round of a six round bout."

I went on to box Brian Husband of Hull twice. Both these fights were incredibly hard, I won the first contest when Husband received a cut eye and the referee stopped the fight. He subsequently had another five fights before our next meeting, winning all of them on knockouts, and a local sports writer described him as a "Dangerous opponent." Our second contest lasted the full distance and when the final bell rang, I was relieved the referee awarded me the points verdict. However the next day my face was so bruised, swollen and tender I could hardly bear to wash.

Chapter 15

The wholesalers, known as the 'Green Market' usually
opened for business at six o'clock every morning and
was always bustling and incredibly hectic as buyers from
shops and large stores, together with street traders, vied
for trade and haggled prices with the vendors. It was so
chaotic it was virtually impossible to find a barrow on
which to stack the purchased sacks of vegetables and
boxes of fruit.

It was on a morning a few days after my second fight
with Husband I was, as usual, buying produce at the
Green Market for my travelling round. After wrangling
and negotiating the best prices for my purchases, I spied
an empty barrow in a corner. Barrows were in short
supply since there were never enough to go round so I

was pleased when I was lucky enough to find one. I walked over, bent down, took hold of the handles and started to push it back to where my provisions were stacked.

Suddenly the salesman who I had bought my supplies from, with a look of horror written all over his face piped up, "Oh, God, take a word of warning from me, don't touch that barrow. It will be more than your life's worth. it belongs to the toughest, hardest barrow boy in the market. Nobody but nobody is allowed to use it but him."

At that exact moment a thunderous voice behind me hollered "Put that f——g barrow back, I'll pull your f——g head off, no bastard touches my barrow, I'll knock your f——g teeth right down your f——g throat."

The voice was getting nearer and louder until he was immediately behind me.

At that precise moment I slowly lowered the barrow to the ground and turned round to face him. He stopped dead in his tracks, apparently recognising me. His face drained of all colour and as he went a deathly shade of grey, he stuttered, "Eee Ron Jackson? Eee I'm sorry, I didn't realise it was you, I saw you fight Brian Husband the other night it was a fantastic fight. I didn't know you came to the market, you can use my barrow any time you like; just take it, any time, any time."

I couldn't help muttering under my breath, "Arse licking creep."

Another morning, having left the greenmarket after

buying supplies from the wholesalers, I was driving my travelling shop down Bath Lane which is in the centre of Newcastle when I caught a glimpse in my mirror of a policeman riding a motorbike following closely behind. He began to overtake and drew alongside my van. He leaned over, thumped twice on the side of the van with his fist, and waved me down to stop.

I pulled over to the side of the road and turned the engine off, wondering what on earth was going on, as I was sure I had not committed any driving offence. I wound the window down and asked, "What's wrong officer?"

He let loose with a tirade of foul language screaming at the top of his voice, "What's f——g wrong? You know what's wrong. You're a stupid f——g arsehole, you're brainless, where the f—k did you learn to drive you f——g idiot? You're a menace, you shouldn't be allowed on the roads."

I began to seethe. My stomach was churning, and I felt incensed at being spoken to like that. Even though he was a policeman, I was on the verge of jumping out of the van to confront him. He must have noticed my fury as he swiftly lifted his visor up to expose his face, whereupon he burst out laughing. He was doubled up and said, "I wish I had a camera, your face was a picture. How are you Geordie?"

Then and only then did I recognise him as a soldier who had served with me at camp in basic training in the R.E.M.E. This was characteristic of him. He was always the joker, always clowning around. We shook hands and chatted for a while before both going our separate ways.

It was a warm summer morning when, after buying my usual supplies at the greenmarket, I was, as customary, driving through the centre of Newcastle heading home. Upon arriving at the Haymarket, I found myself confronted with a uniformed police officer standing on point duty, as in those days it was they who controlled the traffic in the centre of Newcastle rather than traffic lights. The policeman glanced at my van and waved me down to stop, I mumbled to myself, "What have I done wrong this time?"

He came strolling over, gazed at my name on the side of the van, turned around and gestured to the other traffic to halt. "Are you Ron Jackson the boxer?" he asked I said "Yes."

His face lit up and beaming, he said, "I have followed you from the beginning of your career, I'm one of your greatest fans, I have seen every one of your fights at St. James's Hall, I'm so pleased to meet you in person, how are you? When's your next fight?"

After chatting for a moment or two he asked, "What have you got on the van?"

I answered "Fruit and vegetables."

He asked, "Have you got salad?"

I replied, "Yes! I've just bought it fresh from the suppliers."

He asked if he could have a few tomatoes, a head of lettuce, a bunch of spring onions and a cucumber. I jumped out of the cab, opened the side doors of the van to serve him. In conversation, he told me his name was P.C. Dixon and he had boxed as an amateur in the police force.

I began to feel extremely embarrassed, because it being 8.30 in the morning, and peak commuter time; the traffic was building up, I mentioned this fact to the officer but he replied indifferently "Oh bollocks them, they can wait."

After serving him I jumped in and started the van, he proceeded to give me preferential treatment over the rest of the traffic, which by that time, was at a standstill, by opening the way up for me to continue my journey.

About a month later, the van began to give recurrent mechanical trouble with the engine frequently cutting out. One morning after purchasing my goods, I approached Grey's Monument, which is in Newcastle city centre, to be confronted by another police officer on point duty who signalled me to stop. When I took my foot off the accelerator to brake, the engine stopped, consequently when the police officer waved me on, I could not budge. The van refused to start, and was as dead as a doornail. The police officer impatiently gestured again for me to move forward, but of course, it was impossible.

Extremely exasperated he came marching over and shouted, "Get a move on."

I replied. "I can't; the engine's cut out and it won't start; I need a push."

I could not believe it when he obliged; what a sight it must have made, a police officer in full uniform, red faced with physical exertion and perspiring profusely with the effort of pushing a large green three-ton van through the centre of Newcastle. His brute strength eventually paid off, when at last, the van finally leapt into life and lurched forward.

Leaning out of the window, I shouted, "Thanks officer." and drove off, leaving him doubled up and gasping for breath.

Chapter 16

Wyn and I moved into a three bed roomed semi-detached house with a large garden, and it was there our second baby was due to be born on the 9th September 1959. Because Wyn wished for a home birth this time, we arranged for the delivery to be at her mum's house. Wyn was my most dedicated fan and had therefore witnessed all my professional fights. She had travelled all over the country, accompanying me to give her full support, and even though it was extremely close to the day our baby was due, Wyn was determined she was not going to miss my 'Top of the Bill' fight with Tommy Molloy the British Champion, arranged for the 7th September 1959, which was two days before the baby was due. However, our plans were thrown aside when Wyn started to have contractions and went into labour on the 6th of September, the day preceding my 'big' fight. As soon as the spasms began, I drove Wyn to her mum's house and we notified the local midwife who was booked to be present for the birth.

When we arrived at Polly's, Wyn's youngest sister Carole, together with her friend Val, took daughter Yvonne to a nearby park, which was approximately one and a half miles away. This was to keep her absent from the scene, as it would almost certainly be a scary scenario for a three year old to be in the proximity whilst the baby was coming into the world. Our second daughter, whom we named Michelle, was born, early that afternoon. She was perfect, a gorgeous beautiful baby weighing six pounds ten ounces.

The next day, at one o'clock, I attended the weigh-in, for my 'big fight,' to be held that evening at New St. James' Hall. Polly slipped out to the shops for ten minutes to purchase a few baby necessities, leaving Wyn resting in bed with baby Michelle sleeping soundly and daughter Yvonne playing happily in the lounge with her toys. Upon returning home, Polly was shocked to discover Yvonne had disappeared; the panic and distress was unimaginable. I arrived home at the precise moment of the realisation Yvonne was missing, and was met with a distressed Wyn and Polly who were both frantic with apprehension. We began to desperately search for her and I had to restrain Wyn from leaving the house to join in the search, as she was still very weak after giving birth

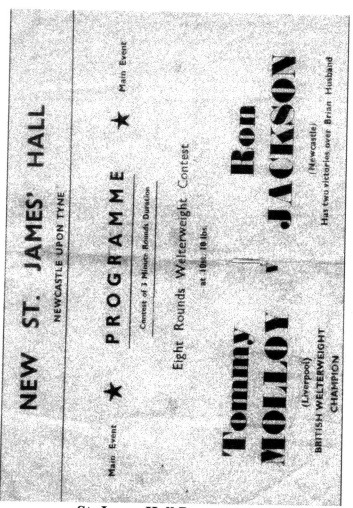

St. James Hall Programme.

a few hours previously.

At that precise moment, Carole's friend Val was on a bus travelling into Newcastle city centre, when she casually glanced out of the window and saw Yvonne toddling along the road. Having been with Yvonne the previous day, Val immediately recognised her so she instantly leapt out of her seat and frantically explained the situation to the driver and requested him to halt the bus, which to her relief he did. She immediately jumped off to rescue Yvonne and, to our immense delight brought her home, none the worse for wear. Yvonne explained she was "Just going to the park to play on the swings."

Apparently, because she had thoroughly enjoyed the previous day she wanted to go again. Our imaginations went into overdrive with thoughts of 'what if' and the realisation of the dangers such a young child could have been exposed to, so were overwhelmed with relief that she was safe.

A few hours after this exceptionally stressful and worrying afternoon, I arrived at New St. James Hall, for my contest with the British champion, the most important fight of my professional career. I struggled to put the nerve-racking events of the previous few hours behind me by pushing them to the back of my mind and climbed into the ring full of confidence. I was aware that I had done very well in the first two rounds, then suddenly in the third round I sustained a very badly cut eye which forced the referee to intervene and stop the fight. Disappointed I made the trip to hospital where they inserted seven stitches into the wound.

Next day, Norman Brown the sports reporter for a local Newcastle paper wrote under the headline;-

Not champion's tactics Tommy Molloy.

"British welterweight champion Tommy Molloy stopped Ron Jackson (Newcastle) after three rounds in Newcastle last night but made himself very unpopular with the Tyneside crowd.

"A left hook cut Jackson's face near the corner of the left eye in the third round and with the blood flowing freely, it is doubtful if the injury could have been patched up to enable him to come up for the fourth.

"However, the champion's tactics incensed the crowd to a storm of booing that brought tears to Molloy's eyes. And he richly deserved the censure.

"He was warned by the referee Jimmy Folland for rubbing his head into the wound and then, only seconds later, he held Jackson with his left arm and cuffed the heel of his right glove across the cut.

"Not the tactics of a champion Molloy! Jackson had done well up to that point. He just shaded the first round if only for his forcing, and some solid straight lefts gave him a share of the second."

I went on to box Brian Curvis who originated from Cardiff. This contest was held at a venue in Liverpool and the bout was scheduled over eight rounds. Unfortunately the fight was stopped in the third round when once again I suffered a very badly cut eye, which being an exceptionally deep cut also required seven stitches. Curvis, my opponent, being a brilliant boxer went on to become British, Commonwealth and Empire welterweight champion.

However, the fight of my career, which sticks predominantly in my mind, must be the contest against Jimmy McGrail at the National Sporting Club in London.

I received a telephone call from Joe Shepherd the Newcastle matchmaker who told me he had arranged a fight for me and went on to inform me of the details of the date, time and venue. Nevertheless when I asked him the name of my opponent, he answered "Mm, I can't remember his name; it's Jimmy something or other."

If only I'd realised, the Jimmy 'something or other' was Jimmy McGrail the fighter whom all the boxing experts were enthusing about, each one tipping him to be the next world champion. He was reputed to be the hardest puncher since Randolph Turpin, and was receiving rave reviews from all the sporting reporters.

Not having the expertise and advice of a manager, and certainly not knowing what was in store for me, I once more considered this an opportunity for a family outing and again hired a car, which was a large saloon. I was driving, Wyn was in the front passenger seat with baby Michelle on her lap, and seated in the back were Ben, and Polly, who had Yvonne sitting on her knee. Also squeezed into the back was my youngest sister Lilian, who was intending to visit Granny Sarah who, after being widowed, had remarried and settled in the capital. When all were safely aboard, we set off to drive to the venue in London.

After completing the long laborious drive, we arrived at London just in time for the weigh in. After all protocol had been concluded, we made our way to Benny's brother's house in Edmonton since he and his wife had invited us all for a meal. Time passed all too quickly and before long I found myself in the ring. I was rapidly to discover the reputation of McGrail's punching power was, regrettably for me, true, and even underestimated.

McGrail fractured my left cheekbone with a right hook in the first round. Nevertheless I tried to battle on courageously, but I was in a hell of a state by the time the referee thankfully stepped in to save me from further punishment in the third round.

In addition to suffering a broken cheekbone, both my eyes had completely swollen up, until they had consequently closed into narrow slits, my nose was bust and bleeding profusely and my lips were so swollen I could hardly speak.

When this punishing, gruelling fight was over, since I was the only person amongst us who held a driving licence, I had to undertake the long drive home. This was beyond doubt, a nightmare. Not only did I have to struggle to see through the tiny slits of my swollen eyes, but unexpectedly, after driving for an hour, we found ourselves in the midst of a dense fog. It was in fact one of the worst the country had ever experienced, and we could only see the diminutive distance of one cat's eye dimly showing through the impenetrable fog.

I managed to tuck in behind a large wagon, to follow the taillights, which being bright red were more noticeable than the indistinct markings on the road. I assumed it must have been travelling north so was quite happy to follow him.

After driving numerous miles, the wagon gradually stopped. I followed suit, and even though we could not see him, the driver climbed out from his cab and approached our car. I was taken by surprise when he suddenly appeared at my window, which I opened. He bent down and said, "I realise you have been following me, but I'm turning off now to drive across country to Liverpool, so if your destination is further north, you're on your own."

We were very grateful that he was kind enough to inform us; otherwise, we would have automatically followed him and would surely have ended up driving a hundred miles or so in the wrong direction. From then on, the driving was even more atrocious. At one point we felt a bump, then a moment later, were stunned to realise we were in the middle of a roundabout. A couple of seconds later another bump, we were off.

Following the horrendous drive throughout the night,

146

it was not until we approached Newcastle that the fog, fortunately began to lift and thanked our lucky stars we had not come to any harm, the only damage being to our nerves, which were completely shattered. I realised the petrol tank was almost empty so I stopped at a filling station on Scotswood Road to fill up.

The garage attendant, who was in fact a pal of mine, strolled over to the car, but because of my injuries he did not recognise me, and said, "Good god, have you been in an accident?"

I said "No just a boxing contest."

He reeled back and gasped "Ronnie Jackson, is that you? It looks like you've been hit with a steam roller."

"It feels like it too." I replied.

After having had 26 professional fights, Wyn and I sat down to discuss my future, and both came to the conclusion it was time for me to retire. I based this decision on the foundation that in my last five successive fights, I had sustained appallingly deep cuts around my eyes. Each time only realising I was severely cut when I felt the warm blood streaming down my face, and became conscious the new cut was more severe than the previous one. Each cut required up to nine stitches, which resulted in bad scar tissue forming around my eyes.

My doctor warned me the protruding scar tissue was a serious weakness and would always cause problems, therefore having my best interests at heart he advised that I should seriously consider retiring. On reflection, he being the expert, I felt I should take his advice and although reluctant, I agreed to hang up my gloves.

Retiring from boxing meant of course I had more leisure time, so qualifying as a 'driving instructor' in the R.E.M.E. I found time to teach Wyn to drive. I had been giving Wyn driving lessons on and off from the time we first met, and she was a very competent and confident driver, so we applied for her to take the driving test. However, on the date the test had been arranged, the only vehicle we possessed was a clapped out old van so Wyn had to take the examination in that.

Because the windscreen wipers on the van did not work, we were hoping for a dry clear day, but fatefully halfway through the test the heavens opened and it started to pour with rain.

Previously I had demonstrated to Wyn, after opening the bonnet, how to tie a connection to the wipers with a piece of thin wire to make them workable.

When the rain started, Wyn apologised to the examiner, jumped out of the van and tried, numerous times to make the connection with the wire but unfortunately failed to get the windscreen wipers to work.

By this time, the driving examiner was furious and exasperated. He hopped out of the van and made the connection himself, unfortunately, during the process, he sustained large stains of black oil on his spotlessly laundered shirtsleeves. Needless to say, Wyn failed this, her first test.

Shortly afterwards we bought an old Vauxhall Cresta car, and Wyn managed to obtain a test cancellation and took a second driving test which she passed with flying colours.

Chapter 17

As mentioned earlier, during my childhood I accompanied father almost everywhere. Now it was my turn to return the favour, and every day I invited him to come along to help serve in my travelling shop. Not only was it companionship for myself, but it also gave him great pleasure to lend a hand, as he being very sociable, thoroughly enjoyed meeting people. He always had a ready smile as he joked with my customers. Since the business transactions were always in cash, each day after father and I had finished the morning round, I give him a few quid out of the takings. Consequently every afternoon he would immediately go to the bookies to have a bet on the horses. Unfortunately I acquired the bug and started gambling alongside him.

Although it became a problem, I never kept Wyn short of housekeeping money and always kept enough money to pay the bills. I would however, gamble the remainder of the takings every day, money which I should have been saving for emergencies, such as cash to repair the van, which was frequently breaking down.

Gambling began to take over quite a large element of my life, and one night I persuaded Wyn to accompany me to Brough Park greyhound racing stadium, and as my van was 'off the road' yet again, we decided to go by public transport and travelled by bus to the Gosforth track. After the dog racing had concluded we left the venue and began to walk to the nearest bus stop. I looked at Wyn in embarrassment and had to confess I had gambled all my money away, so consequently did not even have the bus fare home. I explained there was no other alternative than to walk home. This did not go down too well, but having no other option; we set off, in silence.

Wyn was wearing a new pair of shoes, which had exceptionally high stiletto heels, measuring four and a half inches, so after walking several miles Wyn was almost crippled as she hobbled along, limping badly. I could perceive in her face that every step she took was agony. I felt responsible but the only thing I could offer her was my arm. Eventually hours later, after walking a distance of about eight or nine miles, upon arriving home, she kicked off her shoes and swore, "Never again."

After about a month of trouble free motoring, the van once again developed mechanical trouble and subsequently broke down in the scorching heat of summer. I had just arrived home from the wholesalers after stocking up with boxes of seasonal soft fruits including strawberries and raspberries together with other perishable goods such as peaches, salad food, flowers etc.

Not having money put aside for such misfortunes meant I wasn't able to meet the expense of taking the van to the garage to be repaired; subsequently none of my newly purchased stock could be salvaged and as a result the merchandise rotted in the intense heat. This is where Polly, our guardian angel, came to the rescue yet again. It was a couple of days later when she became aware of my predicament and she instantly insisted on lending me the money to have the van repaired.

I am ashamed to say this scenario actually happened three times in all.

Although I always repaid Polly, Wyn made me recognize my gambling was becoming ludicrous. Therefore I candidly acknowledged I had to change my ways, so when brother Stan who was a foreman plasterer offered me a job, which was extremely well paid, I accepted. Stan was widely recognised as one of the most accomplished plasterers in the whole of the North East, being adept in the most intricate and decorative plasterwork imaginable.

It was after working quite happily along with Stan for several months, that one morning a labourer on the job, named Dennis, came to work relating a sob story. He told us his friend's dog had given birth to a litter of pups five weeks previously. He said his pal had managed to find homes for all of the puppies with the exception of one. Dennis said his pal was going to drown the pup, the smallest, runt of the litter, if he could not find a home within the next two days.

Being an animal lover I was mortified so instantly said "Bring the pup in to work tomorrow; I'll give it a home." Sure enough next morning Dennis arrived with the pup wrapped in an old towel. He carried it over to me but then had the audacity to ask for seven shillings and sixpence as payment. I felt affronted; instead of him being grateful I was saving the pup from the fate of death, he was asking me to pay for the privilege. My eyes narrowed, there was a pregnant silence and I was on the verge of telling him where he could stuff the seven shilling and sixpence, but then I looked down at the pup and felt so sympathetic towards the tiny bundle in his hands, that I relented, and handed over the cash.

I found a cardboard box and made the pup as comfortable as possible on an old jumper of mine, which I retrieved from the boot of my car. This served as a cushion and he snuggled up warm and content, and slept quietly for most of the day, only waking every couple of hours to lap milk, which he devoured voraciously.

After work, I took the pup home and upon seeing the tiny little waif, Wyn instantly bonded with him. We decided to name him Champ. In appearance, he was similar to a smooth haired Jack Russell, although he grew to about twice the size. He was white in colour with brown ears and a couple of small brown patches on his body. In hindsight it occurred to me that it must have been the best seven shillings and sixpence I had ever spent. What an affectionate, obedient little dog he developed into, being totally devoted and loyal to the family and predominantly to daughters Yvonne and Michelle.

I recall one night after we had all retired to bed, I was abruptly woken by a noise, which sounded as if someone was trying to break in through the door at the rear of our house. Instantly, Champ began to bark and growl, therefore I quickly jumped out of bed and sprinted to the door, along with Champ, who had arrived at the scene in a flash. I hurriedly opened the door and Champ, snarling, shot out like a bolt of lightning. Peering through the darkness I glimpsed the shadowy figure of a man disappearing through our garden gate with Champ hot on his heels growling and snapping. It made a hilarious sight, the would be burglar running along the road, as if for dear life, then every few yards he would leap into the air yelling out with pain as Champ jumped up and bit his arse. This continued until he was out of sight. I stood at the gate, shouted for Champ and waited until he came bouncing back along the road, his wagging tail held high. I swear that if dogs could smile he was grinning from ear to ear. He smugly looked up at me as if to say, "That'll teach him; he won't be back in a hurry."

Brother Stan, being a foreman, was in charge of numerous plastering squads, and as a result, during one specific period, he employed father, by giving him a labouring job. Stan at the time was overseeing an important plastering job at a high-class hotel in the centre of Newcastle. The hotel was fitted with an integral dumb waiter used to provide drinks for the guests by ferrying the alcoholic orders up to each level. Each time it arrived at the floor where the plasterers were working it was laden with drinks for the guests, and this was too much of a temptation for father. He could not believe his luck - 'free booze'. Unbeknown to Stan, father helped himself to drinks until he was so much under the influence he could hardly stand. Brother Stan was exceptionally annoyed and humiliated therefore, after receiving a tongue-lashing father was sent home in disgrace.

The next job Stan was supervising was at Prudhoe Mental Hospital. He was in charge of organising the rendering of the entire outside gable end. Stan employed three plastering squads together with labourers and apprentices. He designated me to supervise the labourers and in addition, put me in charge of ordering the required materials.

In conjunction with my first telephone order, I gave instructions for a ten-ton load of sand to be delivered to the hospital at three o'clock on our first working day. Sure enough, the loaded wagon delivered the order exactly on time, dumping the sand in a huge heap as near to the gable end of the building as possible. Virtually the instant the wagon dropped the sand, a male patient who was perhaps in his thirties arrived on the scene with a child's plastic seaside bucket and spade, and proceeded to fill the tiny bucket then disappear. We thought we would just humour him and allow him to continue; he could not do much harm to such a huge pile of sand could he?

However next morning when we arrived at work at eight thirty, we could not believe our eyes, the entire load of sand had vanished, not a grain in sight. Apparently the male patient, together with numerous of his counterparts had worked like beavers throughout the night, not only with buckets and spades but also with shovels and wheelbarrows to shift the huge mound of sand and the mystery was, nobody could locate it. Apparently, it had been finely scattered and strewn over the numerous acres of gardens and grounds within the hospital. The hospital staff were laughing when they explained to us, when seeing the patients apparently having such good fun, and believing it would be a pity to stop them having such rare enjoyment, they decided to turn a blind eye.

Shortly after this, father decided to travel to London to visit his mother, Granny Sarah, father informed mother he would stay in London for the weekend, and travel home the following Monday, so to expect him about teatime.

In those days, it was customary for me to regularly visit mother once a week, and it was about seven weeks after father had left, when I found her frantic with worry, since she hadn't had any communication whatsoever from father. Consequently not knowing whether he was alive or dead, she was astonished when the door burst open to reveal father, stone drunk, who then staggered and lurched across the room to immediately collapse into a chair.

On one hand, mother was relieved but on the other hand, she was, understandably enraged, so began to remonstrate with him; however, he retaliated with a tirade of verbal foulmouthed abuse aimed at mother. I looked down at him with disgust and was furious with him for speaking to mother in that derogatory way. He continued spewing out oaths, so, although not wanting to hurt him, I wanted to teach him a lesson so I bodily grabbed him out of the chair and proceeded to hang him by the back of his shirt, onto a metal coat hook, screwed into the living room door.

It was such a hilarious spectacle, father, his feet about a foot off the ground, his short little legs flailing about in mid air kicking fifty to the dozen, as he dangled, he shouted. "Get me doon yi f——g bastard, get me doon."

He struggled and kicked so violently his shirt ripped open and he dropped to the floor like a stone, muttering profanities under his breath. I warned him to behave himself and said, if he retaliated by taking it out on mother, he would have me to deal with; I left with him still quietly muttering oaths under his breath.

Chapter 18

It was soon after our daughter Michelle was born that Wyn began having problems with her breathing and was subsequently diagnosed as having chronic bronchitis. Even though she had a baby and a toddler to care for, she valiantly struggled on. However, regrettably after a few years Wyn's health deteriorated so much her doctor prescribed steroids, instructing her to take one tablet a day; as a result, she improved for a short period of time.

Unfortunately, the doctor failed to alert her of the dangerous side effects of steroids, so when her breathing worsened and she, not having been warned against doing so, took extra tablets to try to find relief. Eventually, Wyn was taking up to six or seven steroid tablets every day, however, after a while her health worsened so much the doctor sent her to see a specialist at Newcastle General Hospital who was appalled that no one had warned her of the dangers of taking steroids. Subsequently after tests, the specialist told Wyn, that due to having taken excessive amounts of steroids orally, meant that her adrenal glands had either become lazy or had shrivelled up and died, so because adrenaline is absolutely vital for the human body to survive, it was imperative she underwent a course of treatment.

The specialist accordingly admitted Wyn into hospital for a course of A.C.T.H. injections which, we were informed, would make her adrenal gland active again. Wyn was admitted to hospital on her twenty-seventh birthday for, they estimated, about ten days. Since she had never been in hospital before, except for the birth of daughter Yvonne, she was very apprehensive; however, the hospital staff were brilliant. The injections prescribed for Wyn were in the form of a thick gel like substance, stored in a glass container. This bottle had to be heated, to liquidise the contents, before the jab could be administered. One morning, the regular nurse was having a day off and a different nurse was on duty to distribute the prescribed drugs to the patients. This nurse approached Wyn, syringe in hand, preparing to inject her, Wyn, who could not explain why, felt rather uneasy, so asked the nurse if she had melted the contents of the bottle. The nurse looked surprised; she obviously had not read the instructions and said "Oh! I didn't know I was supposed to, that explains why I had to use all my strength to draw the right quantity up into the syringe."

Wyn was relieved she had confronted her; and shuddered to think that it would have taken just as much strength and, would therefore have been excruciatingly painful to have the gel like substance forced into her arm.

Two weeks later, after the treatment had concluded Wyn was very pleased to be allowed home from hospital. However, I was shocked when after only a few days, she collapsed. I frantically called for an ambulance and she was rushed back into hospital, where she lay seriously ill. That first night at hospital, I anxiously waited until at last they allowed me to see her, I was shocked to find Wyn lying deeply unconscious behind curtains which had been drawn around her bed. She had an oxygen mask fitted over her face, and I noticed her skin and lips had acquired a purplish blue tinge.

The doctor had given strict instructions that Wyn must be kept under constant observation. As a result, there was a nurse sitting at her bedside keeping vigil, and a second nurse on hand to take over, so as to give her twenty-four hours care.

The hospital consultant took me to one side and told me Wyn was critically ill and might not survive. Apparently the injections had failed to make her adrenal gland active again and since it is essential for the human body to have adrenaline to survive, the lack of it had caused Wyn's body go into shock. However, to my immense relief, after 36 hours, Wyn began to respond to treatment and regained consciousness. Nevertheless, the doctors said, as a precaution she would have to stay in hospital for twelve weeks.

Wyn was very distressed at the forced separation from our two lovely daughters. Yvonne was eight years old and Michelle was five and had only just started school four weeks previously. In that era, hospital visits by children were not allowed and this truly upset Wyn as being a devoted mum she could not bear the thought of being apart.

The next twelve weeks proved horrendously stressful. I would waken the girls every morning, make and give them breakfast before taking them to Polly's, a distance of about four miles, after which I travelled to work to complete a hard day's graft. In the meantime, Polly escorted the girls to school, then later in the afternoon she waited at the school gates to collect and take them back to her house to eat the meal she had cooked. After work, I drove to Polly's, to wash, change and consume the meal, which she had kindly cooked for me. Afterwards I rushed to hospital to catch the last hour of the strict visiting times, before collecting the girls, taking them home, giving them supper, putting them to bed, and reading a story from their favourite book of fairytales.

We carried out this procedure for twelve weeks solid, and I can honestly say the girls never missed a day's schooling and I myself did not miss a day's work, or a daily visit to hospital.

On a few weekends, I took the girls to hospital to see their mum, but since the wards were out of bounds to children, they were only permitted to stand at the end of the corridor and wave to their mummy. On one hand, this would console Wyn and she appreciated it, but on the other hand, it distressed her, knowing her girls were so near yet so far. However the matron of the ward was an extremely compassionate woman, and a couple of times she secretly allowed Wyn into her office and ushered Yvonne and Michelle in so Wyn could give them a kiss and a cuddle.

Wyn was in a medical ward, which was not as hectic as the busy surgical wards. This meant there were often several beds vacant, which the overflowing geriatric ward quickly commandeered.

This state of affairs was very nerve-racking for Wyn, since the elderly, infirm patients, were placed in beds either side of hers, and as, unfortunately, most of them were terminally ill they died within days.

There was one instance of a very old woman, who occupied the bed adjacent to Wyn's. This old lady was sadly infirm and incontinent, as a result she would defecate in her bed, and then push her hands down under the bedcovers into the mess, bring her hands outside the blankets with fists full of shit, and squeeze the crap through her fingers.

After several weeks of enduring this, Wyn became very depressed and was so desperate to come home, that every day she pleaded with me, making me promise I would take her clothes in 'tomorrow' but of course on the doctor's advice I never did. Disheartened, Wyn threatened to discharge herself, but the matron on the ward took her to one side and made her realise just how ill she had been, and finally persuaded her, for her own good, to stay. The matron kindly offered Wyn a private side ward, which she greatly appreciated, and I am pleased to say it made the remainder of the stay in hospital much more bearable for her.

Finally, after twelve weeks, the doctors were satisfied with Wyn's progress and allowed her to come home. However they explained she would have to take steroid tablets orally every day for the rest of her life.

Regrettably, during the next couple of months, Wyn was rushed back into hospital a further three times, struggling to breathe and because her veins had collapsed through lack of oxygen. Each time the doctors and nurses frantically attempted to locate a vein into which they could inject the necessary medication. I watched as they desperately tried numerous times in both her arms, then, being unsuccessful, they concentrated on the back of each hand, but to no avail.

Finally, after Wyn must have felt like a pincushion they finally succeeded to locate a vein in one of her feet. However once the drugs had been administered Wyn soon recovered and happily after these worrying occurrences, Wyn eventually regained her strength and we slowly got our lives back on track.

Chapter 19

After being employed by Newman's, which was a large plastering firm in Newcastle, for a couple of years, I being very ambitious was itching to work for myself again. At the time I was working with two plasterers namely Eddie Sanderson and Jimmy Brown, and after having several discussions with them, we decided it would be a good idea to become self-employed and start our own plastering business. My first suggestion was to ring the builders who advertised in the Yellow Pages, which is the commercial business directory, to explain we were a newly created firm of first class workers, seeking work and were ready to take on new contracts.

Eddie, Jimmy and I discussed in detail seeking a name

to call our business. We came to a united choice, and made the decision that, since I was the only one of us who had a telephone and transport, and because I lived off a highway called Whickham View, that the name Whickham Plastering Company would be appropriate.

Because I was the one with a vehicle, I collected Eddie and Jimmy each morning to drive around building sites in the area searching for potential work.

One day upon arriving at a site, we were pleased to notice there was a newly constructed bungalow, ready to be plastered. We conversed with the builder and persuaded him to sub-contract the work out to us. He was very meticulous and said he expected a first class job, and would not be happy with anything less. We hastily assured him we were first class workmen and could guarantee he would not be disappointed. After deliberation, he agreed to give us the contract and we went on to complete the plasterwork to the bungalow in record time. Upon inspection of our finished work the builder was very pleased with the quality of workmanship and duly gave us a cheque, asking whom he should make it out to, I replied "Whickham Plastering Co."

After accepting the cheque, we felt jubilant as we drove to the main branch of Barclays bank in the centre of Newcastle, where I proudly filled in a paying in slip, and presented it, together with the cheque over the counter to the cashier, who asked me "Have you an account with this branch?"

I told her "No, but we want to open one."

"Just a moment, I'll get the manager for you," she said.

We explained to the manager we had only just started up in business and he enquired, "Have you registered your company with Business Names?" (Business Names, who on earth are they?)

We of course did not have a clue. He went on to explain it was impossible to pay the cheque into a non-existent account, and advised us to return to the builder, to request a replacement cheque, made out to me personally. This would enable me to open an account in my name and therefore able to deposit the cheque. In the meantime he advised us to register as a company, which we subsequently did.

Since I was resolutely determined to make a success of the business, I was prepared to work overtime every day and to work every single weekend. I also came to the conclusion that I should sell my car to raise funds to purchase a van, as obviously a commercial vehicle would be much more practical.

The three of us continued to work solidly for eight months, then Eddie became cheesed off with the intense hard work and was miffed at having to work so much overtime, so decided he'd had had enough and wanted to quit. We made an appointment with a solicitor who accordingly worked out how much Eddie's share of the profits were, so all in agreement we presented him with a cheque and said our goodbyes.

Several months later, Jimmy too decided that, since having a young family, he wanted to branch out on his own, so as to be able to choose his hours of work, and have more time to spend at home, so he also opted to take his share of the profits and say goodbye.

This left me to cope with the mountain of work single-handedly. Not only did I have to labour to myself by mixing the plaster, but once mixed I had to apply it. I was working seven days a week, without help, plastering walls and ceilings to newly constructed bungalows, so understandably, I was absolutely shattered.

Nevertheless, after a few months of this hard toil, I had saved enough capital to employ a couple of plastering squads plus two apprentices. Things were going extremely well and our reputation as first class plasterers preceded us, meaning the volume of work increased to such a degree that it became more than we could cope with and had to turn down many contracts The fact Wyn was a qualified bookkeeper and therefore able to keep the accounts and invoices up to date, was a boon. She was also responsible for ordering the materials, so was forever haggling with suppliers to obtain the best possible prices, which she did efficiently.

One day I was reunited with my childhood pal, Alan Percival, when out of the blue, I received a phone call from him. Alan after leaving school had served his time as an apprentice painter, then after completing his five-year apprenticeship, he enlisted into the army, joining the Twelfth Lancers for his obligatory two years National Service where he served most of the time on active service, fighting terrorists, in Malaya.

It was not long after Alan had been demobbed from the army that he started his own painting firm. Being exceptionally ambitious, he took no time at all to develop it into a very successful business, employing 42 painters. He was lucky enough to obtain very lucrative contracts, from local councils and schools and was prominent when night clubs began to materialise in Newcastle and acquired all the painting work involved in their construction.

The reason Alan contacted me was to ask if I would be interested in submitting a quotation for the plaster work to a building which was being converted into a night-club, which was the very first to be opened in the centre of Newcastle, it was the Piccadilly Night Club in Bath Lane. I was happy to oblige and submitted a price for the work, which was duly accepted.

On completion of work, the owners of the club organised a pre-opening party night and invited Alan, his wife Anne, Wyn, and myself together with the other subcontractors who had carried out work to the club.

We were asked to meet at the premises at eight o'clock on the Friday night prior to the grand opening of the club. The owners, who were London based, plied us with free drinks all night, and consequently, most of us could hardly stand when the party ended at 6.am. the next morning.

During the course of the evening, the bar staff were concerned about Wyn mixing her drinks. They alerted me after noticing that after drinking a couple of snowballs, she had a couple of brandy and Babychams, before going on to Bacardi and Cokes. However I was not at all alarmed. It always amazed me and I could never fathom out why, but alcohol just did not seem to have any effect whatsoever on Wyn. She might just as well have been drinking lemonade.

Subsequently she was the only one of us still as sober as a judge when they served breakfast courtesy of the club. Many of the painters who worked for Alan told me he was a very demanding boss, which I could quite believe; on the other hand, Alan could be the epitome of kindness.

One example of his generosity is, one Christmas time, he happened to bump into an old school pal, whom he had not seen for many years. It was during their conversation the pal mentioned to Alan that his three young sons desperately wanted bikes for Christmas but unfortunately, as he was unemployed he could not afford to buy them. He was amazed when the next day a van delivered three new Chopper bikes from a cycle shop to his door, presents for the boys, courtesy of Alan. This gesture was typical of him.

I recognised by his determination in his formative years Alan would be successful in life, seeing that, whilst at school he was very positive and had two jobs, one delivering newspapers and the other cycling around the area delivering meat orders for a local butcher. Sure enough, just as I had predicted, he became a millionaire by the age of 35. At that time Alan owned a new Rolls Bentley and would regularly, once a week, pick me up for a lads' night out. He delighted in nothing more than proudly driving slowly through the underprivileged area in which we grew up, secretly hoping our former childhood mates would recognise us.

Occasionally we would drive past someone who, I assumed, upon seeing such an exclusive expensive car must have believed Alan was someone famous or a member of the gentry so would therefore doff his cap. Alan would grin and say, "Bloody creep."

But underneath his hard exterior, I knew he was delighted. In the early summer of 1967 Wyn, the girls and I went to the Norfolk Broads on a boating holiday with Alan and his wife Anne. Alan chose the boat, and of course, it had to be the biggest and the best. The boat, a brand new motor cruiser had just arrived from the boat show in London and we were the very first holidaymakers to hire it. After having the controls explained and demonstrated, we leisurely cruised around until we found a mooring place to tie up.

We secured the boat and Alan and I left Wyn and Anne to unpack whilst we went for a drink to a nearby pub. Surprisingly, we discovered the bar manager happened to be a Geordie who immediately recognised our accents and become very friendly toward us. In conversation, he said, "Forget about Newcastle Brown Ale try this," and handed us two pints of a brew, which was unknown to us.

He said it was so strong that no one had ever been able to drink more than three pints. Alan, being a very heavy drinker, of course had to prove him wrong so downed five, although I myself had only another two halves. It was as we were leaving the pub, the barman said to us, "Next time you're passing, call in and let me know just how you feel tomorrow morning."
We promised we would.

We somehow, with great difficulty and in complete darkness, managed to find our way back to the mooring point. However, as we stepped off the landing stage onto the boat we dropped about six feet to land with a loud clatter onto the deck. We hadn't allowed for the fact that the tide would go out, meaning the boat would drop to a much lower level.

In view of the fact I had only drunk two pints of the strong beer, I was fine the next morning and suffered no after-effects, but Alan had such a mammoth hangover he couldn't even lift his head off the pillow. He lay in bed most of the day, moaning and groaning like a bear with a sore head, and did not feel well enough to venture out of bed until late afternoon. A few days later, since we were passing the same pub, we called in as promised, and on approaching the bar counter, the manager looked at us and enquired, "Well?"

Alan nonchalantly replied, "Oh I was fine; the brew had no effects whatsoever and I certainly didn't have a hangover."

The manager gave me a whimsical knowing look; I winked at him and grinned.

It was I who 'captained' the boat for the first few days and found it exhilarating standing at the helm, steering the boat through the water in the glorious sunshine, whilst the others lounged about and sunbathed on the deck.

Eventually Alan decided he would like to take over; however, by that time it was necessary to fill up with fuel, so we made our way to a nearby filling station. Upon reaching it, Alan began to steer the boat up to the jetty. Regrettably, he had forgotten the procedure of how to stop, (which was to put the gear into reverse). I will never forget the look on the face of the attendant who was signalling us forward with beckoning gestures, directing us towards the fuel pump.

As we approached, our speed was much too fast, so his signalling waves changed to frantic stop signs. Consequently as we continued to bear down upon him, his face transformed and took on a look of sheer terror and he barely managed to jump out of the way, as the boat crashed into the landing stage. The whole fuel jetty vibrated with the collision, which left a gaping hole just above the water line in the brand new boat. When the attendant finally composed himself, he told us not to worry, as the insurance would cover any damage.

It was during the holiday Alan tried to persuade me to go into partnership with him. He pledged to give me fifty per cent of his business and assured me he would buy me a brand new Volvo estate car and give me half of the vast profits. The building trade is notorious for being unstable, therefore having a plastering business, I found I had either far too much work to cope with, or at other times, not enough. I would be dishonest if I said I was not sorely tempted by Alan's generous offer, however after giving his proposal a great deal of thought and after deliberating the pros and cons. I, realising just how very independent I am, came to the conclusion that we, both being on the same wave length would probably conflict over decision making, so declined.

Eventually after a few years, Alan, being extremely wealthy went on to purchase a pub/restaurant at Newton, Northumberland, then a hotel on the Isle of Man, and a pub in Corbridge.

However Alan did everything to excess; he lived life to the full, he drank excessively and also smoked very heavily so regrettably he paid the ultimate price, sadly dying shortly after being diagnosed with stomach cancer at the age of 52.

Chapter 20

One day after sitting down to discuss our future plans, Wyn and I decided it would be in our best interests to buy a house so decided to save for the deposit. Wyn applied for and obtained a job as a part time bookkeeper, and worked during the hours the girls were at school. I myself began to work extra hours, consequently it was only a few months before we realised we had enough money saved for the deposit.

After shopping around the property market and viewing quite a number of houses, most of which were unsuitable, we eventually found the house which was, in our opinion, the most desirable in our price range, we both knew instantly this was the one. The house consisted of two reception rooms, three bedrooms; and had a large lawned garden. The house was one of only twelve houses built in a small quiet crescent shaped cul-de-sac and situated on the outskirts of Newcastle, in a tiny hamlet called Kenton Bank Foot, which consisted of only five roads.

On the late spring day we arrived to view the property, we parked our car on the main road and strolled up the quiet curved cul-de-sac, which was heavily laden with overhanging trees and bushes weighed down with sweetly scented blossom. This made a very good first impression.

We were so impressed with the house and location we immediately made an offer, which to our delight the owner accepted.

Little did we realise, at that time, that finding the right house, and being able to obtain a mortgage, were worlds apart; being self-employed meant every mortgage lender we approached did not want to know and would not even consider our application. This was despite the fact we could furnish them with annual audited accounts, which had been certified by a registered accountant, and submitted to and accepted by the tax inspector for each of the years we had been in business.

Frank Hall was a builder for whom I had worked for over numerous years by plastering the many new houses he built, and with whom I had became very friendly. Frank knew of our intentions to purchase a house, and one morning in conversation, he enquired if I had found anywhere suitable.

I told him we had found the perfect house and went on to explain the difficulty we were experiencing in obtaining a mortgage. To my immense surprise he said. "Don't worry Ron; I will get you the mortgage."

Looking at my stunned face, he informed me he was chairman of Tynemouth Building Society. You could have knocked me down with a feather. I immediately rang Wyn who was at work, to give her the good news and, as expected, she was jubilant. The mortgage was duly arranged and we moved into the house of our dreams within a few weeks, and are forever grateful to Mr Frank Hall.

One period during that first summer in our new house, a builder rang to inform me there was a hiccup in the construction of his next house, which was the next job on my list. As a result, I found I had an unexpected couple of weeks off work. Wyn and I therefore decided to have a long awaited holiday and agreed to hire a towing caravan to drive down to the lovely county of Devon. However, being last minute, August and school holidays this was more difficult than we anticipated.

Wyn rang around the caravan hire firms listed in the Yellow Pages phone directory, but none of them had a caravan available. However, after almost giving up, one of the hire firms said although all their regular holiday caravans were booked out, they did in fact have an old trade-in caravan which had just came into the depot, as a part exchange and agreed we could hire it.

Delighted, we jumped into our car and drove to the showroom to collect it. Nevertheless when we arrived we were very disappointed to find it was ancient, decrepit, tiny and cramped. On impulse we decided it would be better than nothing, at least we would get a holiday.

We hitched the caravan onto our car and drove home to pack, then loaded everything into the cramped space. Wyn, Yvonne, Michelle, myself and of course Champ climbed into the car and we set off. Wyn and I decided to take turns in driving, so I drove for the first four hours, then Wyn took over the wheel. We had just driven through Bristol and were travelling on the M5, heading south. It was very early morning, being about five thirty, so consequently the roads were almost deserted. We were leisurely driving along in the slow lane, driving at about forty miles an hour, when without warning, a huge high sided, box wagon, whooshed past us, so close he missed us by only inches, even though both the middle and fast lanes were completely empty so could have given us a wide berth.

To our horror, we were caught up in the slipstream from his speed, and as a result the caravan began to veer violently from side to side. Wyn had no control over the car, which was swerving erratically, and without warning the caravan overturned and disintegrated into small pieces of debris. Our car came to a sudden halt as we straddled across the three lanes of the motorway, the car bonnet facing the central barrier and the fragmented caravan strewn in a trail behind us.

We scrambled out of the car, and I escorted the girls and Champ as quickly as possible to the safety of the hard shoulder, then both Wyn and I stood in the middle of the road, to wave down and warn drivers of the oncoming traffic to slow down and stop. In the meantime, we spied a police car speeding up the motorway in the opposite direction, lights flashing and sirens blaring. It then crossed through a nearby gap in the central barrier, turned around and came to our aid.

The fact the caravan was ancient was almost certainly the most important factor in saving our lives. The truth was, the metal connection from the caravan had been so corroded it had snapped. Had it been in better condition, it probably would not have broken off and in all probability would have flipped the car over with us in it.

The police were very courteous and sympathetic, as they swept up what was left of the caravan onto the hard shoulder. They informed us that only a few days previously, there had been a comparable accident at the very same spot, but unfortunately, that car and caravan had careered over the hard shoulder to hurtle down the steep embankment. Tragically, the whole family died. We felt incredibly lucky.

One of the police officers, upon recognising our accents, asked, "You're from Newcastle aren't you?"
We replied "Yes."
He said, "You'll be driving straight back then?"
We answered, "Oh no, as we've come this far, we'll just carry on and try to hire a caravan in Devon."

He looked amazed, shook his head and said, "Typical Geordies."

We eventually arrived in Devon and luckily found a bed and breakfast establishment with vacancies, which was very clean and nice; we booked in and stayed there for two nights. In the meantime, we drove around all the caravan sites in the area trying to find one with a vacancy, but we found to our disappointment that they were all fully booked. It was on the third day, when making enquiries at yet another caravan park, the proprietor told us an old woman who lived nearby had a holiday cottage, which she sometimes rented out, and it was possible it would be vacant, so he gave us directions to her address.

We called at the old woman's house and to our delight, the cottage was in fact vacant. She showed us around and then gave us the keys. It was a lovely quaint old building set in its own grounds, which measured approximately one acre.

We found it to be an idyllic spot, with the whole site bordered with rhododendron bushes, which were in full bloom. It was very private and tranquil so we had a glorious relaxing holiday.

The weather was perfect with uninterrupted sun all day long and to put the icing on the cake, the girls discovered a riding school, from which they could hack out across glorious moor land, which of course they did several times. The two weeks passed all too quickly and we soon found ourselves home and back to the slog of work, work, work.

It was shortly after this, that father suffered a major heart attack. He was 63 years old and it happened whilst he was working as a gardener in the grounds of Newcastle's Royal Victoria Infirmary. Immediately after father collapsed, his colleague summoned help to rush him without delay into an intensive care cubicle within the hospital.

The family were instantly summoned, and we immediately rushed to the hospital fearing the worst. Our suspicions were realised when the doctor informed us the prognosis was very grave indeed, and they did not expect father to survive.

The doctor said if his heart attack had occurred any place other than within the confines of the hospital grounds, father would probably have been dead on arrival.

Since the doctors warned us to expect the worst, brother Stan and I decided to keep vigil overnight. As a result, a nurse kindly ushered us into a side ward, which had two single beds; nevertheless, being so anxious, and apprehensive we were unable to sleep.

During the night, each time we heard footsteps coming down the corridor, we thought it must be the doctor coming to inform us that father had passed away. However, being the fighter he was, not only did he survive, but to everyone's astonishment, was back to normal within a few weeks, happily kicking a ball about with his grandsons.

Chapter 21

Champ stayed our loyal companion until, upon reaching the age of 13 years, he regrettably succumbed to kidney failure. it was the week before Christmas, 1970, and understandably, both girls and Wyn were utterly devastated. I myself shed many a tear as I remembered the small wriggling little bundle I had carried home from work all those years earlier.

A few days later, actually Christmas Eve, I arrived home from work only to find the house in complete darkness, which was most unusual, and after letting myself in, I discovered there was no-one at home, so was quite perturbed. It was about an hour later Wyn and the girls arrived home, carrying a huge bundle, which I thought was a curly sheepskin rug, but was in fact a standard poodle puppy. He was a beautiful apricot colour, and only twelve weeks old. Wyn assumed having a new puppy to care for would be good therapy for the girls to help them get over the heartache of losing their beloved Champ.

The pup, which we named Harvey, was very boisterous and extremely large but his fur was so overgrown you could barely see his eyes. As a result, Wyn booked him into a local poodle parlour to have him shampooed and trimmed. When setting eyes upon Harvey, the dog beautician noticed he was a lovely specimen of the breed and suggested Wyn show him. Wyn decided nothing ventured nothing gained so when Harvey was six months old, which is the age puppies are eligible to enter shows, Wyn duly filled in an entry form for a local show, bathed and groomed Harvey and set off full of trepidation.

In this, his very first show, the judge awarded Harvey second place in the minor puppy class, and in his second show, Harvey actually won his class and even went on to win the honour of being Best Puppy in Show. Subsequently Wyn achieved a lot of success showing Harvey who won 'Best in Show' numerous times, receiving cups and trophies, which we displayed on a dresser.

When Harvey was about eighteen months old Wyn received a telephone call from a woman who said she had seen Harvey winning at shows and was very impressed with him. She explained she owned a standard poodle bitch and asked if she could use Harvey as stud when her bitch next came into season. Wyn said, if she sent us her pedigree she would check to see if they were compatible then would decide one way or the other. The next morning the same female rang again and asked Wyn if she would like to purchase her bitch. Coincidentally, Wyn was quite taken with the idea of owning another standard poodle and had in fact been contemplating buying another, so she arranged to visit later that afternoon. This turned out to be quite a distressing experience for Wyn; once inside the house, which was a terraced house in Walker, Wyn found herself confronted with an appalling scene. The woman had five Great Danes which were housed in her back yard, all of which were skeletal in appearance and covered in deep weals and open sores. The woman candidly admitted to Wyn she had numerous cages, which were stacked one on top of the other in the attic room, and each cage contained a toy or miniature dog, which, she divulged, she kept solely for breeding purposes.

Her standard poodle bitch was nowhere in sight, and it wasn't until the woman picked up a long handled broom and poked it behind the settee, that the poodle scuttled out, ran across the room and cowered in a corner, visibly trembling with fear.

Wyn, almost in tears asked the woman how much she wanted for her and feeling desperately sorry for the poodle, she immediately proceeded to buy her there and then.

Being extremely underweight, the poodle was as light as a feather so Wyn picked her up, cradled her in her arms and carried her to the car and placed her on the back seat to bring her home.

As soon as Wyn arrived home, she rang a friend, Dorothy Dixon who was very knowledgeable in the canine world, being a poodle breeder, dog groomer and a Championship dog show judge. Wyn described to Dorothy the scene she had encountered and asked for advice on what steps she should take to alleviate the horrendous conditions in which the dogs were living. Dorothy asked the name and address of the woman, and then informed Wyn she had already been reported to the R.S.P.C.A. and that she was desperately trying to sell off all her dogs before the inspector called. We all hoped she would be banned from keeping animals ever again.

Honey, as we named the poor little mite, was so emaciated her bones were visibly prominent and her hair so badly matted that neither brush nor comb would penetrate the tangles. Wyn who performed all her own grooming and trimming by then, allowed two weeks to elapse, thus allowing Honey to settle in, before putting her through the ordeal of having all her matted hair trimmed off and having a shampoo.

After Honey had been groomed and trimmed, we realised just how eye-catching she was, so elegant and stylish, although she remained extremely nervous and apprehensive until eventually, we gained her trust and confidence. Honey craved affection, and it was not until she realised we were not going to hurt her that she stuck to us like glue. She would cry whenever we were out of sight and she followed me like a shadow and revelled in sleeping on my knee, which she did every night whilst I relaxed watching television.

Eventually Honey attained her ideal weight and her coat grew long and thick, so Wyn began to enter her into shows. Honey excelled herself and won several Best in Shows at huge open shows, with hundreds of entries including champions. However, even right up until the end, if Honey caught sight of a long handled sweeping brush she would tremble with fear and scarper away to find a place to hide.

Over the years Wyn owned nine standard poodles, each with whom she travelled the country, entering and winning numerous firsts at championship and open shows, and each one qualifying for Crufts.

Chapter 22

I take satisfaction in the belief I was, and still consider myself to be, a good dad; therefore, both girls have constantly been able to twist me round their little fingers. When they were young, our schedule was for me to take them to the local stables for horse riding lessons every Thursday afternoon straight after school, and they very soon became smitten with horses and riding. In addition, they had ice-skating tuition with an instructor each Saturday morning and I also took them swimming every Sunday morning.

Life was leisurely moving along, everything was perfect, business was thriving and both girls were obtaining good grades at school and Yvonne even had the honour of being selected as top girl. Shelly being a very good athlete, excelled at sport, and was selected from the school team to represent Northumberland in the hurdle races. She also played tennis, and swam proficiently.

Both Yvonne and Shelly were horse mad, it was when Yvonne was twelve years old, and Shelly nine, they obtained a pony on loan. His name was Duke and they kept him at a friend's farm near Ponteland. Duke proved to be quite a handful; he was relatively wicked and forever trying to buck the girls off. In spite of this, the girls adored him and would ride him at every opportunity, although Wyn and I were quite relieved when after several months, the owner wanted him back.

It was three years later we agreed, after weeks of begging and pleading, to buy the girls a horse of their own. I now jokingly say it was the worst thing we ever did, as it led to purchasing many more horses and involved me in huge expenditure over the years.

One day the four of us travelled up to Scotland to buy Jason, their first horse. He was only two and a half years old and had only recently been transported over from Ireland. He was a bay cob gelding with a lovely temperament, and about fifteen hands high, was a proficient jumper and willing to please.

At that time I did not know what I was letting myself in for. The rounds of gymkhanas and competitions, which occurred almost every weekend, meant extremely early starts.

I had to get up at five thirty a.m. to drive the girls to the stables, because they insisted Jason had to be bathed and groomed before the shows.

We were soon to find out there was a problem with Jason; he loathed going into a trailer. We would sometimes spend hours trying to coax him to walk up the ramp to load. We tried tempting him with food and when this failed we resorted to pushing him, pulling him and then occasionally after all the girls' hard work of shampooing, grooming plaiting etc, they would unfortunately have to miss the event. Eventually when we did arrive at gymkhanas, Jason would excel himself by competing exceptionally well, he won numerous clear rounds, and 'jump off's' against the clock, so many in fact, Yvonne and Shelly's bedroom walls were covered with rosettes most of them red, they being awarded for first prize.

Generally, after the shows had concluded, Jason would, without any encouragement, walk straight into the trailer, I assumed he realised he was going home. On the odd occasion, he was downright stubborn and difficult, and would categorically refuse to box, meaning the girls had to ride him back to the stables, which in itself was very nerve-racking. Although Jason was absolutely bomb proof in traffic, since the gymkhanas were numerous miles away, meant the ride home took ages and the light would sometimes begin to fade as darkness crept in. I would follow closely behind, driving with my hazard lights flashing to warn other traffic, and each time this happened, I said, "Never again."

However, doting dad was always there again the next week.

Yvonne took ten '0' levels, resulting in her obtaining all with excellent grades, so she decided to stay on at school to take 'A' levels, until one day she saw an advert in our local newspaper. "Stables/Riding School to Let."

"Dad look," as she showed me the advert,

"I would love to start a riding school, dad PLEASE, PLEASE."

"What about your education?" I said

"But dad, having a riding school is my ultimate ambition."

Did I mention earlier? - Twist around little finger? I reluctantly agreed to go with Yvonne to inspect the stables, and on examination, we found them to be very nice, but there was one big drawback, in that there was only a small grazing paddock of about one acre. However, the owner of the stables assured us the farmer opposite had agreed to rent a field of about ten acres out to him as grazing for the horses. After deliberation we agreed to go ahead and rent the stables, but of course there was one, or should I say ten, very important things missing -horses.

This is where the nice bank manager came in. I telephoned to make an appointment with him, as I needed to arrange a loan. He was stunned when he knew how much debt I was prepared to accumulate for my daughter, but he readily agreed to give me assistance to finance our project, smiling he said to me. "You're a wonderful father; not many men would do as much."

Finance agreed our next undertaking was to select and purchase the horses. We rang the horse dealer from whom we had originally bought Jason, to enquire if he had any others, which would be suitable for riding school purposes. He informed us he had just received a consignment of horses and ponies from Ireland, which would probably be appropriate.

As a result, we drove to Scotland, where we chose and purchased four; a beautiful chestnut horse, a stunning dun horse, a lovely chestnut pony and a cute steel grey pony. The various other horses and ponies we purchased were acquired locally. All were vetted by the local veterinary surgeon who passed them as being fit and safe for a riding establishment; we therefore duly obtained the compulsory licence from the local authority.

Yvonne left school and undertook the demanding responsibility of mucking out stables, feeding, grooming and tending the horses. She worked very hard to build up the riding school, and Shelly assisted after school and at weekends. As knowledgeable riders, they both taught youngsters the basics of riding, and in addition they accompanied experienced riders when hacking out along the nearby bridle paths, so soon built up a good clientele.

If the weather were nice on the days when there were race meetings at Newcastle racecourse, Yvonne would close the riding school and we would set off for a day at the races. Since Yvonne and Shelly were not very interested in watching the races, they spent most of the time, gazing longingly at the magnificent thoroughbred horses being paraded around the paddock.

It was at one of those race meetings, they noticed and were enamoured with a beautiful filly being paraded around the paddock. Her name was Quendon. She was a three-year-old dark brown bay and her coat was gleaming like satin in the sunlight as she proudly pranced around the ring, prior to running in the following race, which just happened to be a selling race.

During the race, Yvonne and Shelly were shouting encouragement and willing Quendon to win, and indeed, she ran a very good race, subsequently finishing in third place. However it was very close, the distance between the winner and Quendon being only three quarters of a length.

Immediately after the race both Yvonne and Shelly seemingly disappeared into thin air, only to reappear about half and hour later, excitedly rushing back. Apparently, they had assumed, because Quendon was in a selling race, the owner must be willing to sell her, so had therefore approached the trainer to ask if she was for sale. They explained enthusiastically to us."The trainer said he will ring the owner to ask if he will sell her to us.""Oh! DAD PLEASE, PLEASE."

Now when have I heard that before?

I went in search of the trainer and eventually found him working in the box in which Quendon was stabled. By then he had already contacted the owner by telephone, and informed me the owner was indeed willing to sell her, but upon hearing the asking price, I almost keeled over. I said the price tag was far too exorbitant, and told the trainer I could not possibly pay as much and went on to explain Quendon would never be raced and would only be kept as a fun horse for the girls to ride personally. The trainer made a note of our telephone number and said when he returned home to Newmarket he would have a word with the owner, and get in touch if he were willing to drop the price.

A few weeks passed, but to the girls' disappointment, the trainer hadn't been in contact. However one morning they noticed an advertisement in the local newspaper, which was promoting a blood stock sale, apparently the first ever to be held at Newcastle racecourse, so the girls obviously wanted to go.

"Just to look." they said.

As I was leaving for work on the morning of the sale, I gave strict instructions - "NO MORE HORSES, just window shopping right?"

"Yes dad," they said in unison.

Looking longingly at the blood stock horses being auctioned, Shelly spied a thoroughbred yearling filly called Jenny, who was an exceptionally fine-looking specimen and even at her tender age was already over fifteen hands high. Shelly pleaded with Wyn to bid for her. Wyn at first hesitated, but since she is just as soft as myself, she consented. Ultimately, Jenny came into the parade ring and the bidding commenced. The girls were constantly badgering Wyn to, 'keep on bidding', although every time the price increased she was uncertain as to whether to place a higher offer, but when hesitating, she was prompted by an elbow being nudged into her ribs. Finally, her bid was eventually accepted, but Wyn did not know whether to laugh or cry.

Problems yet again. Jenny obstinately refused to go into the trailer to be transported to our stables, even though there were four hefty men trying to coax and coerce her into the box. Because they were unsuccessful Shelly and Yvonne had to walk from the racecourse in Gosforth, leading Jenny by a head collar and lead rein to the stables near Dinnington which was a distance of eight miles. This was a dangerous procedure, since the only route to follow was along main roads and it being commuter time, the roads were hectic with heavy traffic, so a very anxious Wyn drove her car slowly behind with hazard lights flashing.

Then, to the girls' delight and to my utter dismay, the very next morning, Quendon's trainer rang to say the owner had agreed to sell her at a price, which was acceptable to me. He explained he could convey her

198

from Newmarket up to Newcastle, 'In two weeks time.' Since he would be transporting other racehorses which were entered in races at the next Newcastle meeting, he said he could deliver her right to our stables at Dinnington. Because the girls were jubilant, I didn't have the heart to refuse, so made the relevant arrangements to meet the trainer on the specific day of delivery, to escort him to the stables and take transfer of ownership of Quendon and to give him a cheque.

Every week, we would ask the owner of the riding stables, when the field opposite was going to be available for grazing, but he always fobbed us off with one excuse after another, until eventually, after becoming desperate to obtain grass for the horses and ponies we went to see the farmer ourselves. Upon enquiring about the grazing, he was dumbfounded, and denied any knowledge of ever promising the field; in fact he said that there was no way he would allow horses onto his land saying "Horses are far too destructive; they are notorious for breaking fences, and after periods of heavy rain they churn the ground up."

Had we been aware of this fact at the onset, we undoubtedly would not have entered into an agreement to rent the stables.

This left us in a dreadful quandary. All the money earned in the riding school was being consumed on outgoings. In addition to rent, which of course had to be paid every week, the horses had to be fed, and as working horses, they needed not only the best quality hay, but also hard food. In addition, there were blacksmith and vet's bills to be paid. This of course meant every week we suffered a shortfall of quite a large sum of money.

Winter came and regrettably, hay became very scarce, as apparently, since we had endured a dreadfully wet summer, most of the hay, after having been cut was ruined by torrential rain as it lay on the ground. Subsequently we found it extremely difficult to obtain enough to feed the horses.

As our supply was getting perilously low, Wyn searched through the Yellow Pages' and rang all the farmers within the vicinity to enquire if they had any spare hay for sale. Starting with the letter A she went alphabetically through the directory getting more concerned as the answer was always the same, "No, sorry we haven't any."

Eventually, almost to the end of the alphabet, Wyn upon reaching the letter W, spoke to a Mr Raymond Wright of Ponteland who said he did in fact have some hay. He explained it was not great, but would probably suffice.

Feeling a sense of relief we drove to the farm to inspect the hay. Consequently we met the farmer Mr Wright and his wife Mame' who were a lovely elderly couple.

The hay, as Mr Wright (Raymond) said was not

brilliant but it was better than nothing and we were only grateful we had at last managed to obtain some. Raymond said his nephew Gordon would deliver the hay by trailer whenever we needed it, and this he continued to do until finally we ceased running the riding school.

We hung on as long as possible for the sake of the girls, but soon realised we were plummeting deeper and deeper into debt, so could not possibly continue. Consequently, after months of struggling, we reluctantly decided we had no option but to close the riding school and sell the horses. After their initial disappointment the girls were delighted that most of the regular riders who they knew and trusted, offered to buy their favourite horse or pony. Knowing they would be well looked after, and cared for, softened the blow for Yvonne and Shelly. Yvonne kept Jason, the first horse we had bought for them, and also Quendon, while Shelly kept Jenny who by now was two years old.

Chapter 23

When we first visited Raymond and Mame at their farm, we noticed there was an old dilapidated stone building opposite, which was set in a paddock of almost three acres of land. After we had relinquished the riding school, we asked Raymond if he knew who owned it, and if it might be for sale, since the property was the exact type we were looking for - one with a grazing paddock for Jason, Quendon and Jenny.

Raymond informed us the property belonged to him, and said over the years, he had been persistently pestered by numerous people, who upon seeing the derelict building when driving past, would stop, call at his house and try to persuade him to sell it. This irritated Raymond, and since he was very suspicious of strangers, he always declined.

We were delighted and felt very privileged when Raymond told us he would very much like Wyn and I to become his neighbours, so would apply to the local council for planning permission to convert the ruined building into a house. Since the building had previously been used as a dwelling, there was no problem with obtaining approval for the renovations. We were to discover the old stone building was in fact The Water Mill of Kirkley. We both being very interested in its history visited the local records office and traced The Mill back as far as 1523. At that time it belonged to a Lord Ogle, and seeing it was already constructed, it was obviously built prior to that date.

On agreeing to purchase The Mill from Raymond, we commenced the renovation work in September of 1975. This was a major undertaking as the building was so dilapidated, part of the roof had caved in, and also the old stone walls were crumbling. At some period during the previous years, The Mill had been converted into a cow byre, involving the construction of stalls and floor being created out of reinforced concrete, which were understandably extremely difficult to break up. We used sledgehammers combined with pure brute force to complete the demolition. Whilst working on The Mill, we found a half sovereign coin, in absolute mint condition, a lovely keepsake for Wyn who had it mounted onto a gold chain to wear as a medallion.

Dilapidated Mill, Kirkley.

I was misguided in my belief we could complete the renovation of The Mill and have it ready to occupy within three months, as even with all my staff, who helped by working overtime each day and weekends, six months had passed and it was still unfinished. However, since we had sold our house at Bank Foot and obliged to vacate the premises by the 1st March 1976, we decided to move into The Mill, even though it was still far from being ready. At that point in time, we were not connected to any of the main services, so did not have electricity, water or heating. There were also gaping holes in the walls, made in preparation for the windows, which were yet to be installed.

Raymond kindly allowed us to store most of our furniture and belongings inside one of his large outbuildings, with the exception of the bare necessities needed, i.e. beds, clothing and kitchen equipment, which we moved into The Mill.

On the day we moved into The Mill, according to the weather reports, it was the coldest March day the country had experienced for numerous years, the temperature being at least ten degrees below freezing - this in itself was certainly an endurance test. Yvonne and Shelly stayed for one night only, then understandably, because of the adverse freezing conditions they said they could not tolerate it, so went to live with Polly. Each morning I filled plastic containers with drinking water and carried it from Raymond's farm which was on the other side of the road. We used candles as lights and purchased a camping stove so as to heat water, soup, beans etc. A friendly neighbour, Mr Hedley who owned a farm further up the road, kindly loaned us a paraffin heater. However since the staircase had still to be fitted, we had to make use of a long ladder propped against the first floor landing, to enable us to climb up to the bedrooms. Finally after a few weeks the restoration work had been completed and the house was completely refurbished so at long last Yvonne and Shelly could return to their new home.

The next project, which we felt essential to undertake, was to immediately construct stables for the girls' horses, I therefore set about building them, and on reflection, we realised if only this property had become available whilst we were running the riding school, it would have solved all the problems we had confronted and would have been just perfect.

Yvonne was lucky enough to find a good job and began full time employment in the offices of British Telecom, whilst Shelly was still studying at school. We soon found, because our property was situated three miles from Ponteland and there being no public transport, meant either Wyn or myself had to shuttle Yvonne and Shelly to work, school and all social outings.

Shortly after we had settled in, and wanting to be

independent, Yvonne took a course of driving lessons. She had just turned seventeen and because she picked up the fundamentals rapidly, her instructor said she was a natural so immediately applied for a test. Yvonne was lucky enough to obtain a cancellation and fortunately, as expected, she passed her driving test first time. This made Shelly very enthusiastic to learn to drive. However being only fourteen, she was too young to obtain even a provisional licence, so I offered to give her driving lessons in our three-acre paddock. Shelly jumped at the chance and indeed learnt the basics very quickly and became a proficient driver in no time at all; I placed obstacles in random positions, for Shelly to manoeuvre around, and she conquered these hurdles with ease.

I usually drove Shelly to school every day, and it was one morning she asked if she could drive the van up the road. Because the road to The Mill is an unclassified road and all those years ago, was extremely quiet and only used occasionally by the odd farm vehicle, against my better judgment, I agreed. In hindsight, I should never have allowed it, but dad being dad crumbled, and as usual gave in to the request from daughter.

Off we went. Shelly at the wheel driving the van up the winding, twisty, narrow road, and doing exceptionally well, when having almost reached the top of the road, we were unexpectedly confronted by a police car, which was driving towards us from the opposite direction. Shelly being so tiny was conspicuous as she could barely see over the steering wheel, and I noticed the police officer was frowning and looking perplexed as he drove past us.

Fully expecting the policeman would want to ask questions, I assumed we would, without doubt, be in deep trouble. However, I felt safe in the knowledge that he would have to go a long way down the road, before finding a space wide enough to turn his vehicle. I watched him in my mirror, and the instant he disappeared from sight, I ordered Shelly to stop and rapidly changed places with her. I took over driving and upon arriving at the top of the road, I speedily drove into Mr Hedley's farmyard, situated, on the left-hand side, and concealed the van behind his large hay shed. Shelly and I jumped out of the van and furtively peeped around the corner to watch and wait until the coast was clear. A moment or two later the police car came speeding up to the junction and we secretively watched as the policeman stepped out of his car. He seemed confused as he looked right then left, he scratched his head, mystified that we were nowhere in sight. He then climbed into his car and drove away.

Next morning, being Saturday, I was working as usual in the garden, when a police car pulled slowly up to the fence. The same police officer who had passed us the previous day, stepped out and beckoned me over.
"Is that your van?" he enquired pointing over to it.
I answered, "Yes officer, it is."
"Who was driving it yesterday morning?" he asked.
"My daughter Yvonne." I replied.

"How old is she?"

"She's seventeen, but don't worry she has a full driving licence."

Frowning and showing signs of disbelief, he requested to see her licence, I walked into the house and since I was aware of the exact drawer in which Yvonne kept her licence, I singled it out to show him.

He scrutinised the licence and said "Yes that's O.K. but could you please clarify one thing, which has been puzzling me? Which way did you turn when you reached the top of the road yesterday?"

"We turned left," I said casually.

He climbed back into his vehicle and drove away.

Phew!

One day Yvonne arrived home from work and said, to my surprise, "Dad, I've been pressurised into entering an 800 yards race."

Apparently, British Telecom, for whom Yvonne worked, was organising an open sports competition, to be held at Gateshead International Stadium. I was surprised to say the least, as the only sporting activity Yvonne had ever shown any interest in was horse riding.

I explained she would have to train exceptionally hard, to attain the goal of getting herself in shape and supremely fit for the event, and seeing as there were six weeks until the day of the competition I offered to coach her. Yvonne was more than happy to agree, so as a result, we began our regime of training, and began to run and jog early each morning before work. The first two weeks, we ran just two miles daily, sprinting the last 100 yards, then we stepped the training up another level, increasing the distance and the sprinting. Subsequently I initiated endurance training, running at first six miles, then ten miles, sprinting further and faster each time.

Ten days before the race meeting I took Yvonne on a 13 mile run, and then gradually reduced the running back down to two miles. I told Yvonne to rest for the final three days so she lounged about the house, either reading books, or watching television. Consequently, on the day of the competition she was as fit a fiddle, and said she felt like a time bomb waiting to go off.

On the morning of the race, upon arriving at Gateshead Stadium, I bought a programme and noticed most of the eight runners in Yvonne's race had an asterisk next to their names. I asked an official what this meant and I was informed it meant they either were international runners or had represented their county in the event. My stomach sank and I was very apprehensive, as this was the first race in which Yvonne had ever competed. Before the race I gave Yvonne strict instructions, "Stay on the shoulder of the leader, and on the last bend give it everything you've got."

The starting pistol fired, and Yvonne carried out my

instructions down to a T as she shadowed the leader, and then on the last bend, she burst forth and ran like the wind. She passed the leader with ease and was pulling further ahead. Excited, I leant forward and hollered at the top of my voice "GO ON YVONNE."

A woman who was standing immediately in front of me nearly jumped out of her skin. I apologised for giving her such a fright then proudly explained it was my daughter. Yvonne won the race by at least two yards, and to put the icing on the cake, she had broken the British Telecom record, which was a great achievement. I felt especially proud, as my daughter had excelled herself by defeating several international athletes.

The girls often travelled into Newcastle city centre for a night out with their friends, so either Wyn or I had to shuttle them back and forth. This meant driving them into Ponteland to catch a bus into town, then, because the last bus was at eleven o'clock, one of us drove into the centre of Newcastle, usually at about two o'clock in the morning to pick them up.

One specific night, in the depth of winter, February if I recall, Yvonne decided to catch a bus home from Newcastle, consequently I arranged to pick her up in Ponteland at eleven o'clock. As the weather was simply atrocious, it being almost a whiteout with huge flakes of snow falling. I decided it would be safer to drive the van rather than the car, and as I had just finished a job the

Yvonne

van was laden with heavy tools and wooden scaffold, I therefore assumed the weight would be much safer for road holding in the treacherous icy driving conditions.

Whenever I picked either of the girls up, and because their safety was always primarily in my mind, I arrived at the bus stop ten minutes early; to make sure I was already waiting when the bus pulled in, especially in the darkness of winter.

This specific winter night, I sat patiently waiting until the bus pulled into the bus stop. Yvonne jumped off and came running over to the van. However as she was doing so, a police car stopped next to me, and the policeman opened his door, climbed out and walked up to my van.
He looked into my window and said, "Do you know are committing an offence?"
"No officer, how?" I asked.
"You have pieces of wood, in excess of the allowed length, protruding out of the back doors of your van," he said.

With that, I leapt out of the van, and untied the knots from the rope, which held the back doors together. I reached inside, picked out a saw from amongst the tools, and then proceeded to saw off the offending two feet of protruding wood. I collected the off cuts of wood, then together with the saw, threw them into the back of the van, closed the doors then said,
"Is that all right officer?"

He burst out laughing, Yvonne who had been standing watching in amusement just said "DAD, "in exasperation.

Daughter Shelly also obtained very good grades at school, and was subsequently accepted for college. She moved out of the family home to live the typical lifestyle of a student, sharing a house which was divided into rooms, with other student friends. She dressed in the characteristic student fashion of the time, with clothes almost touching the ground, and laced up Dr. Marten boots. The room Shelly rented was on the ground floor of a large three-storeyed house. She kept her space clean and tidy although it resembled a jungle, with large plants and cacti, for which she seemed to have a passion.

You couldn't say the same for the other student tenants. Upon entering the front door, the pong that hit you was appalling. The reason being, numerous turds of cats' faeces, just left to rot, on the stairs leading to the upper rooms, and the stench of cats' urine was overwhelming. This together with discarded, empty beer cans and bottles undeniably made the place into a tip.

Shelly has always been a very independent person, and would not accept any financial help from us, she would regularly assure us "I'm fine, I can manage."
It was only afterwards we found out she was sometimes so hard up, she could only afford tinned pea sandwiches for dinner.

Shelly went on to buy a motorbike, which, as

parents, made us very anxious and concerned for her safety. After owning a couple of smaller bikes she saved up to purchase a huge, one thousand c.c. bike. Shelly is tiny, being just over five feet tall and about seven stones in weight, therefore, since the bike was so powerful and bulky she looked like a little doll sitting astride it, but that was characteristic of Shelly - she prefers the biggest horses and the biggest bikes.

Wyn and I were relaxing in the house one day when a policeman came knocking at the door. He enquired if we had a daughter called Shelly, and seeing our anxious faces, full of dread and apprehension, he quickly assured us there was nothing wrong.

Apparently he had seen Shelly riding her huge motorbike and had followed her in his car. He had assumed it was a young boy and far too young to have a licence, so he believed the bike must have been stolen.

Accordingly he had stopped Shelly by waving her down, and was flabbergasted to discover it was indeed a young lady.

The police officer told us he was routinely checking to confirm if the details she had supplied him with were true, and we of course assured him they were.

The next Sunday happened to be Mother's day and Wyn and I were working in the garden, when we noticed Shelly riding down the road on her motorbike. She was grinning broadly, and as she pulled up outside the gate she proudly reached behind to retrieve Wyn's present,

Shelly

which was strapped onto the back of her bike. The present had started as a beautiful large flowering plant, but, after a journey through wind and speed, the leaves and flowers had long disintegrated, meaning the only thing left was the stalk. Shelly's face dropped with disappointment and then we all burst out laughing.

Yvonne became a vegetarian in her early twenties. Being an animal lover she couldn't bear the thought of them being killed for consumption, and she had also watched a horrendous programme on television about the horrific slaughter and transportation of animals which involved significant cruel practices, making her determined never to eat meat again. I myself had never been comfortable eating meat, but had the misconception that meat was vital to maintain health and strength. I held these views until I watched a documentary on television, relating to the Silver Backed Gorilla. The programme stated that they are the strongest animals on earth, even though they are strictly vegetarian.

I immediately converted to being a staunch vegetarian, and have never ever eaten meat since. Wyn followed suit about two years later, and Shelly and her family became vegetarians at approximately the same time.

Chapter 24

When quietly reflecting, I can recall numerous hilarious incidents, which occurred during the years I was in business including the following.

At one particular time, it was imperative I acquire another van. As a result I set out to see a mate who owned a spare parts/scrap vehicle depot, knowing he sometimes sold vehicles which were taken in to his yard to be scrapped. However upon finding, in his opinion, they were not beyond redemption, he would repair them to sell on.

As it happened, on the day I called, he had taken in an old Bedford van, which he said he had checked over and was O.K., so I proceeded to buy it from him.

A couple of weeks later when I was dropping Yvonne

off at school on my way to work. I felt a small jolt and thought I had just driven over a bump in the road, so ignored it, then instantaneously I noticed a wheel rolling past the van. I did not put two and two together and nonchalantly said to Yvonne, "Oh look there's a wheel!" She replied, "YES DAD, IT'S OURS."

The realisation hit me: - as the van slowly slewed into the nearside kerb, scraped along for a few yards, then toppled over onto its side. My first thoughts of course were for Yvonne. Thankfully, she was safe and unhurt, although visibly shaken. I jumped out of the van to retrieve the wheel, which was lying flat on its side, several feet further along the road. A number of youths who were passing, volunteered to help me push the van upright. Once this was accomplished, I began to search the ground for the wheel nuts, but unfortunately could only find two. I proceeded to jack the van up and fitted the wheel back on. However I was conscious having only half the nuts which were required to secure the wheel safely on would be a hazard, so I drove very cautiously to school, dropped Yvonne off, then made my way to a nearby tyre depot, to purchase replacement nuts.

I pointed to the wheel nuts to illustrate to the tyre fitter which ones were required. He slowly walked around the van, gazing intently at the wheels, then a startled expression of amazement swept over his face. He turned and shouted to his fellow workers "Hey! lads, cum ere haav a luk at this."

They wandered over and crowded around the van, then

all burst out laughing.

I asked "What's so funny?"

The fitter enquired "How on earth did you manage to get around corners?"

I said, "Why do you ask?"

He replied, "Your van's got four different size wheels."

I was dumbstruck; no wonder the van was so cheap. It was no coincidence the wheel had dropped off and neither wonder the steering had felt peculiar. I was obliged to purchase a new set of wheels, which cost much more than the price I had paid for the van.

The next amusing incident that comes to mind is, when I was working for a local builder Bill Coulson, with whom I became very friendly. At the time he was building extensions and kept me particularly busy, as I was his main plastering contractor. One night, Bill rang to inform me his next job, which was in fact a bedroom above a garage, was ready to be plastered. During our conversation Bill warned me the lady of the house was 'Odd and very strange.' He went on to advise me to "Just humour her; you will understand what I mean when you meet her."

I together with my squad of plasterers and labourers arrived at the house at eight thirty on the morning we were to commence work. The woman opened the door and showed us upstairs to the extension, and very kindly offered to make us tea or coffee, offering to lace it with whisky or brandy. I declined gracefully, saying work and drink do not mix, but we would be very grateful for a cup of tea at eleven o'clock.

No sooner was the work under way, than the woman came into the room with a bucketful of hot water, a scrubbing brush and several floor cloths.
She asked, "Do you mind if I clean up whilst you work?"
I said "No of course not."

I did not expect her to literally get down on her hands and knees and to crawl about on the floor immediately beneath us. It is commonly understood whilst plasterers are working, it is inevitable quite a lot of plaster drops off their trowels, so because I was concerned for her, I warned her that she would get covered in plaster. She looked up, smiled and assured me that she was all right, stating "I don't mind at all."
As anticipated, she, being directly underneath us, was being rained on with great dollops of plaster and dirty water. In no time at all she was covered with muck from head to toe. However she was adamant and stubbornly insisted she continue with the cleaning assuring us, "I'm all right."

Next morning, we arrived at her house to skim the extension, and found the floor had been scrubbed excessively. It was so spotless you could eat your lunch off it. I explained to her it would become just as filthy again, but she assured me it wasn't a problem, so we experienced the same scenario over again.

Another amusing episode was that, when I had completed a job and consequently informed the owner of the house how much he owed me for the work, he enquired, "Have you any children?"

I said, "Yes I have two daughters."

He instantly disappeared, only to reappear five minutes later pushing a Silver Cross high pram.

He said, "Will you accept this instead of money?"

I looked in disbelief and said to him "My daughters are grown up."

He said "Well, you can take it to a second hand shop."

This infuriated me, I thought to myself, this bastards taking the piss, so I curtly said, "You take it to the second hand shop; just give me the money you owe me."

I think he must have taken one look at my face and recognised just how annoyed I was, he disappeared returning ten minutes later with a cheque.

I refer next to a job at a large detached house, which was being altered and modernised. The owners were extremely wealthy, and very well spoken, they, as we say, "Spoke wi marbles in their moothes."

In all honestly they were an exceptionally nice couple and very friendly towards us tradesmen.

The lady of the house told the workmen everyone must be on 'first name' terms.

One morning she came through the door into the room in which we were working. She was frowning and looking puzzled, and said to the joiner "Who told you to fix the door on that side of the frame?"

223

The joiner answered, "Your husband."

She shouted, "WHAT?" "Don't take any notice of that idiot; I make all the decisions in this house, in future refer all queries to me."

With that, she angrily flounced out.

The builder, Bill, grinned, and said to us, "Her husband is only one of the top surgeons in the Newcastle General Hospital."

It was a couple of days later that she ordered her husband to go to the local hardware shop for several items which were required, one item being, a new wheelbarrow.

He said "But dearest, I won't be able to get it into the car."

She looked at him in frustration and replied, "Haven't you any sense at all? Surely it is obvious, can't you use that small brain of yours? Walk to the store, buy the items, place them in the wheelbarrow and push it home."

"Yes dear." he submissively replied.

He dutifully went about his task, and upon arriving at the shop, he bought the wheelbarrow then accordingly filled it with the sundries and trundled home. Well it was only two miles.

Yet again, we were working in a beautiful house, this time on the Darras Hall estate, a very exclusive area. The owners were having an extra bedroom and bathroom extension built. Unbeknown to us, the lady of the house had arranged for an electrician to come to fix the wiring the following day.

I apologised and explained to her there was no way we could complete the job by the end of that working day in readiness for the sparky, but would definitely finish it the following day. She began to plead with me, begging us to stay to complete the work. She suggested that I ask one of my lads to work overtime, saying she would give him a lift home. Mick, one of my plasterers, reluctantly agreed to stay back to complete the job.

Next morning when I picked Mick up, he said to me "Ron, if she asks again, I'm not available."

I asked "Why"?

He said, "Talk about a stomach churning drive! No sooner had we driven out the gate, than she began driving at 70 miles an hour, then as soon as we reached the main road she began to drive so fast we were touching 100 miles an hour. Never again. I've never been so terrified in all my life."

I smiled and could only assume that she must have been showing off in her brand new powerful Jaguar.

It was later that morning, when, no sooner had the plumber finished fitting the bath, and the electrician had completed the wiring, than the lady appeared, wearing a bath robe. She immediately went into the bathroom and started to run the water, and it wasn't long before we heard her splashing about as she bathed, singing at the top of her voice. The workmen thought this was hilarious, as the bathroom looked like a bombsite, being completely bare, the bath being the only piece of equipment fitted.

Fifteen minutes later, she came out of the bathroom draped in her robe, with a towel wrapped around her head and started relating a tale. She gave a good impression of an actress on centre stage, with us, the unlikely audience of scruffs, about eight of us in all, rough and ready tradesmen and labourers, sitting together on the floor eating our bait.

Her arm outstretched she began, "Picture this in you minds, (pause) just imagine a cruise ship, sailing the Mediterranean, I came up from the ballroom and strolled onto the deck in my evening gown. It was a warm balmy evening, I caught sight of him, he was casually leaning against the rails, wearing a tuxedo. The moonlight was shining on his face, he was so tall, so handsome, as I strolled towards him, our eyes met, it was so romantic. You've met my husband haven't you?"

We had of course seen her husband; could this be the same man? He certainly was no oil painting; in fact, he was downright ugly, a chinless, weedy skinny bloke; how we stopped laughing I do not know. We were biting our lips until they were almost bleeding, as we tried to avoid eye contact with each other, then almost immediately she left the room, someone turned the volume of the radio up as loud as possible and we all rolled about the floor splitting our sides laughing.

It was just before Christmas when a builder rang me

and asked if I could do a small job for him. Although we were extremely busy at the time, because he was a good mate, I said I would fit it in.

The plasterwork to be carried out was in a greengrocer's shop in Whitley Bay, and on the morning we arrived, we were met by the shopkeeper who told us he did not want to close the shop, because he was afraid he would lose business. He went on to explain he had covered half the shop with dust cloths and covers and asked if we could plaster it in sections.

This was proving particularly awkward, having to manoeuvre around boxes and display shelves, but we were in fact managing, only just. Then directly before lunchtime, a lady customer came into the shop with a little West Highland White dog on a lead. She was probably in her late fifties, and resembled a typical English ma'am, attired in a tweed suit and wearing thick woollen stockings. As I squeezed past, carrying a hand-board full of plaster, the Westie suddenly lurched forward and growling ferociously, bit me on the ankle. As this was so unexpected, I jumped with shock and the hand-board of plaster was thrown up into the air, the plaster flew off and splattered all over the lady customer and her little dog. She screamed with annoyance and stamped out of the shop, shouting as she left, "I'll never ever come into this shop again."

I looked at the shopkeeper and apologised saying "I'm really sorry about that; I've lost you a customer."
He grinned and said, "You've done me a big favour; she's the customer from hell. I have been trying to get rid of

her for months. She is forever complaining, she moans and grumbles about all the produce. She returns fruit and vegetables demanding replacements, and is always criticising the prices. I should be thanking you."

Next day was Christmas Eve and traditionally in the building trade, workers cease work at lunchtime. Therefore, when it reached twelve o'clock, we started to clean up and to pack our tools away. The shopkeeper noticed we had stopped working and asked in horror "Oh! You're not leaving now are you?"
I said "Yes we're finished for the holidays."
He replied, "But there's not much work left to do."
I said "There's about two hours work left."
He implored. "Please stay, I really need the work finished so that I can clean up over the holidays."
I answered "Well! It's up to the lads; if they are willing to work we'll stay."
The shopkeeper turned to my two lads, Mick and Billy and beseeched them saying "If you stop to finish the job lads, I'll really make it worth your while."

Mick and Billy pushed the thought of going to the pub to meet their mates for a pint or two, to the back of their minds and instead, thought of Christmas spirit, goodwill to all men and all that. Not forgetting of course the promise of extra cash, which would come in very handy for the Christmas holidays. After a moment's deliberation, they agreed to stay to finish the work.

It took the three of us just under two hours of hard, non stop graft, to complete the work, and when we had finished, I informed the shopkeeper who said "Just a minute lads."

Expecting they would probably get at least a fiver each, they watched and waited in anticipation as he walked away. A moment or two later he reappeared and said to Mick and Billy "Thanks lads, I really appreciate you staying back to finish the work so I want to show you my gratitude."

With that he placed an apple into each of their hands;

They both seemed to go rigid with disbelief as they looked down at the apples in amazement, then as if shell-shocked, they walked like zombies out of the shop.

Once outside Mick said, "I don't know whether to eat it or frame it!"

I could not help laughing at their perplexed faces; the thought of Scrooge was utmost in my mind as I said to them "Well they are lovely red ones."

Being good lads, they quickly saw the funny side and it became the main topic of conversation on the way home. However, I felt so sorry for them that I gave them extra money in their pay packets to make up for their disappointment.

I wouldn't ordinarily work away from home, however one night, a friend rang to say he was desperate for a team of good plasterers to travel to Edinburgh and plaster out a shop which he was refurbishing and developing into a boutique. I had completed several similar projects for him over the years, as he had refurbished and opened quite a few shops in Newcastle and he twisted my arm until finally he persuaded me to go.

I decided the van would be too slow and cumbersome to drive all the way to Edinburgh, therefore I decided to take our car. Wyn and I had purchased a Ford Escort only two weeks earlier, and up to that point, it was the best car we had ever owned, since all our previous motors had been old bangers. However this car had only three thousand miles on the clock and was in spanking new condition.

The five of us, two plasterers, two labourers, and myself, made an early start and consequently arrived in Edinburgh at eight thirty in the morning. After an exceptionally hard day's graft, we made our way back to the car park in Princes Street, in which we had parked the car; however after a thorough search, we were unable to find it. Puzzled, we began to think that maybe we were in the wrong car park, so began to search another one nearby; however, to my dismay there was no sign of it there either.

At that moment, I assumed it must have been stolen, so we made our way to the police station, which was just around the corner, and reported it missing.

The police officer on duty said, "I can guarantee you'll never get it back. There is an organised gang in the area stealing cars, and the Ford Escort is their prime target."

Subsequently there was only one thing for it; we would have to catch the train back to Newcastle. The five of us felt so uncomfortable as we boarded the train; we were covered in plaster and so dirty that the grey plaster dust billowed off us in clouds as we sat down. We were also laden with dirty buckets, full of plastering tools and brushes, and to make matters even worse it was a busy train full of commuters. I could not help but feeling acutely embarrassed.

The Scottish police officer was correct in his prediction, we never did get the Escort back, and unfortunately had to wait several weeks before the insurance settled the claim thus allowing us to purchase a replacement.

Chapter 25

Life was ticking over, boxing and army days just distant memories, therefore being so busy with my plastering business I hardly had time to give the past a second thought, when, out of the blue, in 1977, my sister Eleanor rang to ask me if I would manage her son Alan.

Alan Robertson was an accomplished, successful, amateur boxer who had trained with the England squad. Sister Eleanor said that over the previous weeks, he had thought long and hard, and had come to the decision he wanted to turn professional, but said he would only do so if I would agree to be his manager. Alan at the time was 23 years old and was married to Ethel his childhood sweetheart, who said she was willing and happy to support him every step of the way in his desire to become a professional boxer. Knowing Alan was a dedicated, committed boxer, I was confident he would give his all, and train with enthusiasm. I therefore agreed, saying I would be pleased to train and manage him, so I applied for and obtained a Boxing Manager's Licence, consequently a new phase of my life was set in motion.

My father was very proud of Alan who was in fact his first grandson, so I involved him in all of our training programmes. This gave father a new interest in life and he helped at the gym by timing the rounds and helping me with the corner work.

Alan effortlessly obtained his professional licence and was soon to make his mark in the professional ranks as a first-rate, strong, fit and aggressive featherweight; Alan was well known as a crowd pleaser and quickly moved up the ratings to take his place amongst the top ten featherweights in Great Britain.

I believe the highlight of Alan's professional career must be the night he beat Pat Cowdell, who at the time was being groomed to fight for the world championship, and up to that night was undefeated, and therefore rated 'number one' in the country. The contest was held in Cowdell's hometown of Wolverhampton and of course he, being the local fighter, was favourite and expected to win, but his fans didn't envisage Alan's determination as he purposefully advanced out of his corner, with one thing in mind and that was to win. He made his

Alan Robertson.

intentions known as soon as the contest began and achieved his objective when he stopped Cowdell in the second round.

Newspaper Quote:

"Alan Robertson a 23-year-old plasterer who has a chance of becoming Britain's next featherweight boxing champion took a significant step towards the title when he rocked the boxing world with a second round win over Olympic bronze medallist Pat Cowdell."

Newspaper Quote:

"A tough counter-punching Geordie, Alan Robertson halted Pat Cowdell's charge up the fistic ladder when some savage punching stopped the Warley feather weight with a cut eye at the end of the second round."

It was a night, a few weeks later when a well-known British promoter rang me to request that Alan box on his next promotion, which was to be held at a top hotel. This was to be a 'catch weight' contest meaning Alan had to lose four pounds to make the weight. Nevertheless, even though Alan trained especially hard, we found unfortunately, when we arrived at the venue for the weigh in, Alan was still two pounds over the agreed weight.

The promoter was infuriated, and demanded Alan go down to the boiler room, which was in the basement of the hotel, to 'skip for an hour' to lose the extra two pounds. He, as you would expect, provided the skipping rope and personally escorted Alan, together with my father and myself down to the boiler room. He stood and watched as Alan commenced skipping, but because the temperature in the room was utterly oppressive and the sweltering heat unbearable, he left us to get on with it.

Realising if Alan continued, he would be as weak as a kitten for his fight, so immediately the promoter was out of sight, I ordered Alan to stop skipping, and opened the doors to allow some cool air into the room and I told Alan to sit down and rest.

When the hour was almost up, I located a two-litre bottle of spring water, which was packed in our training bag and sprinkled it all over Alan to drench him, thus simulating perspiration.

Father was standing at the door, keeping lookout, and warned us as soon as he heard the promoter approaching and I immediately instructed Alan to quickly resume skipping.

Upon entering the boiler room, the promoter took one look at Alan and when seeing he was wringing wet, was consequently satisfied he must have lost the excess weight. Smiling to ourselves, we made our way to the dressing rooms to rest until Alan's fight. However, we were extremely disappointed when Alan lost the bout on points.

Immediately after the contest, we made our way to our hotel room, so Alan could shower and change before travelling back home, and had only just let ourselves into the room, when unexpectedly, the telephone rang. I answered and was surprised to hear it was the promoter, requesting I go instantly to his hotel room. I took the lift up to the appropriate floor, knocked on his room door, and heard his voice shout, "Come in."

As I stepped into the room, I became aware it was occupied with not only the promoter, but also with six of his boxing associates and hangers on. No sooner had I taken a couple of steps over the threshold, the promoter started to hurl a tirade of abuse at me, screaming obscenities, and referring to Alan being two pounds overweight.

He yelled at the top of his voice, "Call yourself a f——g manager? You couldn't manage a f——g whore house, I'll have your f—— —g licence taken off you, and I'll sue you for every f——g penny you've got."

I heard his colleagues, sniggering in the background and the blood slowly drained from my face. A red mist slowly descended over my eyes. I was incensed, nobody, but nobody speaks to me like that, I lunged forward, grabbed him by the throat with my left hand, pushed him up against the wall, and pulled my right fist back into position. At that moment a couple of his mates rushed forward and grabbed my arm to prevent me striking him.

Slowly calming down I growled to the promoter, "Don't you ever, ever f——g speak to me like that again."

I turned and left the room, slamming the door so hard it almost came off its hinges.

As I waited for the lift to go downstairs, still trembling

with anger, I was aware of someone coming up behind me. This person followed me into the lift and I realised it was another boxing promoter who had been present in the room, and witnessed the whole incident. He leant forward, patted me on the back and said, "Well done Ron! I've never ever seen him handled like that before. Everyone is shit scared of him; he treats everyone like scum. That's the first time I've ever seen anyone stand up to him."

Still feeling livid, I completely ignored him and did not reply.

Back home, and expecting repercussions relating to the promoter's threats, I was almost speechless when the following week, he rang and greeted me with a warm friendly "Hello Ron, how's things? I'm looking for a fighter to box on one of my promotions next week; have you anyone available?"

You could have knocked me down with a feather; I can only assume I must have gained his respect, because from that moment on, I found he began to give me preferential treatment, by quickly admitting us into venues, instead of us having to wait outside to go through the normal protocol of being identified. Also on each future occasion, he gave us the best dressing rooms.

It was because Alan was so successful that other boxers approached me to request that I manage them also. As a result the next boxer to join our stable was Jackie Dinning, who himself was a useful little flyweight. However since there were very few flyweights in the country at that time, we regrettably only managed to match him with a few fights.

The incident I remember mostly concerning Jackie was, when a local businessman namely Jimmy Stanley, was endeavouring to raise money to donate to the local N.A.B.C., so had subsequently arranged to fly Muhammad Ali from America to the North East. He consequently organised for him to box an exhibition bout with Richard Dunn at the Washington Sports Centre. Jimmy rang to ask me if I would allow Alan and Jackie to box a few rounds in an exhibition contest on the same bill. Knowing it was for a charitable good cause, I readily agreed.

Upon arriving at the sports centre on the night of the exhibition bill, the three of us were strolling down the corridor, when I noticed walking towards us, was my old pal Richard Dunn. He greeted me with enthusiasm, and said "I thought you'd be here, I've been looking all over for you. Come into my dressing room, I'm sharing it with Ali."

The dressing room was heavily guarded with security men; however, we were allowed to follow Richard in without being challenged.

Once inside we noticed Ali, surrounded by all his entourage including his wife, and although we had seen photographs of her in the media and therefore knew she was a striking woman, we were more than impressed when coming face to face with her. She was an astonishingly, stunning statuesque woman, who stood over six feet tall, and had the persona of a top catwalk model.

Jackie had the audacity to approach Ali, and in his broad Geordie brogue confronted him and asked "Di yi mind, caan a hev me pickcher taakin wi yor lass?"

I can only assume Ali in all probability did not understand one word Jackie had said, as he just nodded his head.

Jackie was euphoric and immediately advanced towards Ali's wife, he slid his arm around her waist, then grinning from ear to ear, he proudly posed for a photograph. It made an amusing sight, since Jackie is only about five feet three, so she was consequently towering above him. I glanced across at Ali, who seemed oblivious to the event; he was sitting motionless, eyes focused on one spot, as he seemed to be meditating. After the photograph had been developed, Jackie proudly strutted around showing it to all and sundry.

The next boxer to join my stable was Derek Nelson, a light welterweight from Sunderland, who was a very talented clever, boxer/puncher, who, with dedication could quite easily have been British champion. Being extremely elusive he was very hard to hit, meaning that after thirty-two professional fights, he was virtually unmarked, and didn't have any of the normal trade marks which pugilists usually suffer after having had a professional career, such as a bent nose or thickened eyebrows.

It was after having about twenty fights, winning most, that Derek was matched to fight the Belgian Champion, in his hometown, which of course gave the Belgian an advantage. It was arranged for Derek and myself to be flown from Newcastle to London, and then to catch a connecting flight over to Belgium where the promoter had arranged for a taxi to meet us at the airport to take us to the location of the weigh-in, and subsequently transport us to our hotel. The driver, who spoke English, was to be our interpreter.

Upon arriving at the hotel, which was a small elite establishment, we found we were treated with exceptional courtesy and kindness, Derek and I were introduced to the chef, who said we could choose anything we craved from the vast menu which he presented to us. We scrutinized the incredible cuisine and Derek selected lobster as his main course, followed by a knickerbocker glory; he found the food so scrumptious that he asked for 'seconds'. The chef, on being informed I was a vegetarian, cooked a special meal for me, which was mouth-wateringly delicious.

Subsequent to dining, we were escorted to our luxurious room to unpack. However when we glanced out the window, we observed that immediately across the narrow street, and therefore in close proximity to our bedroom window, was a quaint old church.

Then to our dismay, every hour on the hour the church bells pealed out thunderously. They clanged to such an extent the whole room seemed to shake with the vibration. Consequently, that night, we didn't have much sleep - was this a coincidence? Or was it a scheming ploy on their part? If it had been the latter, it did not work, because after a cracking fight Derek won the contest on points.

Next to join, our camp was P.T. Grant (Paul Tucker) a local boxer who had previously travelled down to London to turn professional. However once there he felt disillusioned, and believed he was being used only as a sparring partner, so decided to return home to Newcastle, and request I manage him.

It was after one of Paul's fights, which had taken place in Glasgow, that, when travelling home, we decided to stop at an overnight motorway cafe for a coffee and a snack. It was late, about one thirty in the morning, and as we approached the counter there didn't appear to be any staff on duty; in fact there was no one in sight. I tapped on the counter several times, trying to attract attention but to no avail. I glanced over to Paul, who was standing further down the counter, and to my disbelief, I saw that he was slowly moving along the 'help yourself' counter, and at each section, he lifted up the food guard, took a portion of food out and tasted it. First he took a large bite out of a couple of sandwiches, put them back, he went on to take a bite out of a pie and did the same with a cake. I could not believe what I was observing and shouted, "What the hell do you think you are doing? Cut it out Tucker."

He laughed and replied, "Don't worry Ron; they'll just think they've got mice."

That was typical of Paul always the joker.

Another local boxer to join our camp was Norman Morton. Norman, a light welterweight, was a fitness fanatic, who always trained to a level of supreme fitness and went on to box, top of the bill, at the National Sporting Club in London.

It was at the National Sporting Club, another boxer of mine, a lightweight. Billy Smith fought a local Cockney lad. This was a very close contest and although I knew Billy had scraped through, I was expecting a 'home town' verdict, but to give the referee credit, he gave the decision to Billy. However, on returning to the dressing room, we were confronted by a particularly irate brother of the opponent, who was extremely intoxicated. To my horror, he pulled a knife from the inside pocket of his jacket and moved towards Billy in a threatening manner.

Instinctively, without thinking what the consequences might be, I threw myself in-between them and managed to defuse the situation and calm the brother down, who turned away mumbling oaths under his breath. I just hoped his next target was not the referee.

In addition to training hard at the gym, the boxers travelled to my house at weekends, for intensive training, and since we lived three miles from the village of Ponteland, we were surrounded by fields and narrow country roads. Myself still being very fit and active would train equally with the boxers, however the most arduous task of all, was running through ploughed fields. We would find each step would gather heavy clay and mud onto our boots, until we would end up with enormous bulbous feet, so weighty we could hardly lift them off the ground.

One day I received a telephone call from a boxing manager, John Spensley who was based in Middlesbrough. He had just signed a contract to manage a boxer called Howard Mills, who had recently moved into the area from the Midlands. John Spensley asked me if I would train Howard, as he was living in digs in Newcastle. I agreed and arranged for Howard to come to my gym. Howard was a part-time fashion model, and was most impressive, being tall with an amazingly good physique. On the first night he walked into our gym, he was dressed in an eye-catching white suit, and wearing a black trilby hat, looking every bit the model he was.

It was understandable my boxers, being rough and ready Geordies, and who were all wearing old baggy tracksuits, wringing wet with sweat, started to take the Mickey out of him, and all through the training session, they goaded him with quick retorts and jokes. However being good natured he took it all in fun.

Many years later I was saddened to hear, that, apparently during a dispute at a nightclub in the centre of Newcastle, at which Howard was employed as a doorman, he regrettably, because of the conflict, had been shot in the leg, resulting in the amputation of the limb.

It was an evening at one show, in which several of my boxers were performing, that Ernie Evans, a pal from my far away army days, walked into the dressing room. I was flabbergasted and so pleased to meet up with him again after 30 years, we embraced each other and shook hands vigorously. Ernie being an avid boxing fan, began to come to my gym several times a week, to observe the lads training. He also accompanied us to all the boxing shows.

Since there were no boxing promotions in or around Newcastle at that time, we consistently had to travel to venues from one end of the country to the other for contests. Considering I was anxious for Paul, (P.T. Grant) to box for the Northern Area Light -Heavyweight Championship I realised the only way to accomplish this was to promote a show ourselves. Consequently, Ernie and I, after several discussions, decided to promote a boxing show in Newcastle, and jointly, share the expenses and costs.

As a result, Ernie and I began to look for a suitable venue in which to hold the promotion, and in the meantime we designed the bills and programmes. We arranged for a championship belt to be created especially for the event. It was made from broad red leather and incorporated a descriptive engraved brass plate, and would accordingly be presented to the winner. We arranged for the mandatory publicity to advertise the boxing programme with the local press, and subsequently went on to hold a successful show in November of 1981, the location being the 'Bier Keller' in Waterloo Street, which was situated in the centre of Newcastle.

Paul's opponent was a pugilist named Reg Long and the contest was scheduled over ten rounds. After a hard bout, Paul clearly won the title on points, and the championship belt was duly fastened around his waist as he euphorically held his arms up into the air with delight. It was three month later, February 1982, Ernie and I decided to promote a second show, the venue once again to be held at the 'Bier Keller.'

Paul was to top the bill for a second time. However the moment the fight commenced, it was apparent to me Paul was evidently 'out of sorts' since he didn't appear to have the usual buoyant persona which he usually portrayed throughout his fights. Working in Paul's corner during the minute break between rounds, I was consistently enquiring if there was a problem, but Paul vehemently insisted he was fine.

I myself was not quite reassured, and although the fight went the whole scheduled eight rounds, sadly, Paul lost the bout on points.

Back in the dressing room after the contest, as I was undoing the bandages from his hands, Paul collapsed onto the floor doubled up in agony. I instantaneously called a doctor, who immediately, packed him off to hospital, where Paul, after examination, was diagnosed as having kidney trouble, and was therefore hospitalised for several days. The truth subsequently came out, he had been plagued with kidney problems since childhood, but Paul had concealed this information from me, and had also kept the fact a secret from the boxing medical board so as to obtain his licence. This of course put an end to his boxing career.

Paul is now a professional actor, performing under the stage name of Paul Palance. He has had several speaking parts in numerous television programmes, and had a major part in a 'one off episode of The Bill. In addition, Paul has performed in a couple of the Catherine Cookson's novels, which have been serialised. He also played the character of a boxer who challenged Zack Dingle to a fight in the T.V soap, Emmerdale. To my amusement, Mandy Dingle knocked him clean out. I will not let him live that down, tough Paul, P.T. Grant, being K.O'd by a girl!

Chapter 26

Wyn retained her job, working part time as a bookkeeper, for a year or two after we moved into The Mill, then, since she was tired of travelling to an office in the centre of Newcastle each day, she decided to give up work. However, seeing she had always been a very active person, she became extremely bored after a few weeks. Subsequently after careful deliberation she considered starting her own business, "To give me something to do," she said.

Wyn decided that being an animal lover, and since she seemed to have an affinity with dogs and cats, the idea of starting boarding kennels and cattery seemed the best proposal. Since we had plenty of land on which to construct the buildings, I agreed with her, even though I

249

anticipated it would mean more work for myself.

Wyn unassisted designed and created the layout and style for the kennels and cat pens and passed them to a local architect who drew up the final plans. We duly filled in the application forms and applied to the local authority for the compulsory planning permission, which we were soon to obtain. Subsequently, with the help of local subcontractors, we constructed the new buildings and had our project up and running within a few months.

Wyn was extremely happy managing the business as she adores caring for animals, and being able to work at home was a bonus. When the kennels were initially launched, I assisted Wyn by helping to walk the dogs before I went to work, then after a hard day's graft I would come home to help walk dogs once again.

Subsequently after a couple of years in business, being a small establishment and therefore not having enough facilities to cope with the demand for extra bookings, by our growing list of clients, we extended the kennels and cattery. Because of the increase in business, it was imperative we employed staff; this meant that, fortunately, I was relinquished from having to walk dogs twice a day.

Over the years, Wyn developed the kennels and cattery into an exceptionally good business with faithful clients swearing they would never go anywhere else. They trusted us and knew we, as genuine animal lovers, would always put their pet's welfare above anything else. However tending and caring for other people's beloved pets is a very responsible and nerve-racking occupation. We would frequently lose sleep worrying over the welfare of the very elderly dogs or cats, or at other times, be extremely anxious if any of the pets appeared 'off colour'. Occasionally, we would have a dog or cat boarding with us who seemed distressed and therefore would not eat. This caused great concern and Wyn spent extra cash buying best quality steak and chicken for the dogs and salmon, tuna and cod to tempt the cats.

Our staff had strict instructions that, when walking dogs, they had to keep a safe distance between each other. We recommended to the kennel maids at least twenty yards apart would be appropriate. We found occasionally, dogs could be very aggressive towards each other, even if they appeared to be very placid in the kennels; therefore, it was imperative there were no calamities.

I recall one incidence, when a black Labrador called Ben came to our kennels, just for the day, as his owners had been invited to a wedding. They brought Ben to our establishment at nine o' clock in the morning and arranged to collect him at five o' clock that same afternoon; they requested we did not feed him, as they did not want to change his diet.

Later that afternoon while the kennel staff were walking dogs Wyn and I were in the office, when suddenly we heard an awful commotion. Full of apprehension we ran out, only to discover Ben had dragged his kennel maid over to the other side of the road and upon reaching another kennel maid, without warning had lunged forward and seized the small dog she was walking, by the scruff of the neck.

Wyn and I were mortified as we dashed forward to give assistance; Ben refused to relinquish his grasp, no matter how hard we struggled. I tried to physically force his mouth open but to no avail, so Wyn, out of desperation, grabbed Ben's balls and squeezed hard, he understandably yelped and instantly let go. Wyn was so concerned for the little dog, she did not give her own safety a second thought, who knows, Ben could quite easily have turned to attack her.

Trembling with emotion, Wyn scooped the little dog up into her arms and rushed into the office where she expected to discover the dog to be bleeding and injured, but upon thorough examination we were astonished to find there was not a drop of blood in sight, and no sign of any injury whatsoever, not even a tooth puncture mark - the little dog's neck was only wet with saliva.

About an hour later, Ben's owner called to collect him and when we explained what had happened, he laughed aloud and explained, "Well there wouldn't be any injuries. Ben has had all his teeth extracted, and he could only have sucked him."

He explained that, in the past, Ben had attacked

several dogs and was in danger of having to be destroyed, therefore to save him; he decided the alternative of having all his teeth removed would be the easiest solution. If he had only told us when he brought Ben to the kennels, it would have saved us the worry and torment we had experienced that afternoon.

Another incident which comes to mind is when Wyn took a booking for a four-month-old Doberman puppy from the owner who asked if he could bring him immediately. An hour later upon arriving at the kennels, the owner seemed very despondent and explained his wife was refusing to keep the puppy, who was called Max. The owner explained his eighteen-year-old son had purchased the pup without his mother's consent. There had not been a problem at first because his son had been unemployed and could take care of the pup himself.

However, his son had found full time employment and because both he and his wife were also in full time work, meant Max, the pup, was left in the house unattended every day, from eight o'clock in the morning until six o' clock in the afternoon. Consequently when they arrived home from work, the house was in a dreadful state, as Max being only four months old, had understandably fouled and pee'd all over the floor. Being confronted with this awful mess on numerous occasions, his wife said Max had to go, saying if the puppy was still there when she arrived home from work that afternoon, she was leaving; she was adamant and refused to spend another night in the house with Max. The owner asked

Wyn if Max could stay at our kennels until he found him a new home. Wyn willingly agreed, and although Max was not house trained he was a lovely natured pup, and since he was eager to please and willing to learn Wyn spent quite a number of hours training him with some success.

Six weeks later, the owner rang explaining he was desperate because all his efforts to re-home Max had been fruitless. He asked if we ourselves could help in trying to re-home him. After making several futile phone calls, Wyn decided to contact a local newspaper, which kindly ran a feature story in which she appealed for a home for Max. The newspaper printed a photograph of him sitting next to Wyn, which brought a response from a farmer who lived in a hamlet near the village of Ponteland.

The farmer, together with his wife, made an appointment to come to see Max, explaining they already had a Doberman bitch, but because she was lonely, they wanted a companion for her. Max was such a handsome specimen, but even more important was, he had a lovely temperament.

The farmer seemed very impressed with him and informed us Max would have the run of the farm. However this concerned Wyn, who was fearful Max, being very young, would chase his sheep. However, the farmer put her mind at rest by assuring her they did not keep sheep, saying they were purely 'dairy' farmers.

Nevertheless, Wyn also had a niggling suspicion that

MAX LOOKS FOR A NEW HOME

Max.

they, having a bitch, might have only wanted Max as a stud dog for breeding, so explained to them the market, at that time, was saturated with Doberman puppies. She advised them to look through the adverts in the pets' columns of the local newspapers and they would see they were filled with litters of Doberman puppies for sale. They assured Wyn they definitely had no intentions of breeding from their bitch, therefore Wyn rang Max's owner to inform him about the offer of the new home and requested him to make the final decision.

He at once agreed that it sounded the perfect home so Max was duly driven away in the farmer's Range Rover.

Max seemed to settle into farm life really well, Wyn who had grown very attached to him, kept in contact with the farmer just in case there were any problems, then after a few weeks she, together with daughter Yvonne went to visit him at the farm. Max appeared to be perfectly happy. He had grown a couple of inches and his coat was gleaming; this reassured Wyn and she came home happy.

Several months went by, then one day Wyn rang the farm to enquire how Max was doing, only to be stunned on being informed by the farmer's wife. "My husband had to shoot him; he went on the rampage killing several lambs."
Shocked, Wyn said "But you said you didn't keep lambs."

Farmer's wife:– "We don't, but he went through to the neighbouring farm, and Oh by the way, our bitch had ten pups and you were correct, we advertised and re-advertised them but in the end, only sold three, and by that time they were nearly four months old so my husband had to shoot the other seven."

Wyn felt nauseated with disgust and put the phone down, and cried herself to sleep that night.

Chapter 27

Raymond and Mame' were lovely neighbours, who to their great disappointment had not been blessed with children. They compensated by possessing two dogs and numerous cats, which they regarded as 'their babies'.

Each summer, Raymond spent hours in his beloved garden, growing vegetables, salads and fruit, and every summer he would present us with buckets full of fresh garden produce, which he placed outside our door several times a week. This was greatly appreciated, as the taste of fresh produce is much superior to shop bought merchandise. I returned the favour be doing odd jobs and plasterwork to their farmhouse whenever required.

Raymond was a poultry farmer, who had been in

business for numerous years. However it came to the point when he realised he had had his fill of all the hard work and all the hassle being self-employed brings, so decided to retire. Raymond owned several acres of land, which he decided to sell, so a near neighbour bought about thirty acres from him and we ourselves bought the twenty-five acres, which adjoined our original paddock.

It was shortly after Raymond retired Mame' developed cancer in her lower jaw, which necessitated in her having to have a major operation, whereby the surgeon removed the cancerous bone and transplanted one of her ribs into her jaw.

Almost every day, Wyn drove Raymond to hospital to visit Mame' as since his eyesight was deteriorating, he was not very confident driving. We felt this was the least we could do to help them in their hour of need.

Eventually Mame' was discharged from hospital but as she was unable to chew, her food had to be pureed. Raymond cherished Mame and looked after her every whim. Wyn called each day to enquire if there was anything she could do to help and took them shopping every Friday so they could purchase their weekly groceries.

It was on one of her daily visits, Mame' told Wyn, Raymond had severe pains in his chest, but had obstinately refused to allow her to call the doctor, claiming he was fine.

Wyn was particularly concerned, and tried her best to

persuade and coerce Raymond into receiving medical attention, saying it was essential a doctor examine him, but he adamantly refused, saying, "If I'm no better by tomorrow morning, then I'll agree to see the doctor."

Being enormously worried for Raymond's well-being, Mame' and Wyn were apprehensive, thinking 'Tomorrow might be too late,' so decided, against Raymond's wishes, to call the doctor anyway.

The doctor upon visiting, advised it was imperative he be admitted to hospital immediately, but Raymond stubbornly refused to go. It was eight o'clock the next morning, and just after I had left for work, that Mame came across to our house.

Upon opening the door and seeing how distraught Mame was, it was obvious to Wyn something was dreadfully wrong. Mame whispered, "Wyn, I think Raymond is dead - will you come over?"
Because Wyn had never ever seen a dead person before, it was quite harrowing for her, and was made even more traumatic since Raymond had died sitting upright on the edge of the bed, with his eyes wide open.

Wyn helped Mame to lay Raymond down on the bed, and then she summoned the doctor, who diagnosed Raymond had died of a massive heart attack. Wyn assisted Mame as best as she could, by helping her with everyday chores.   She also administered the daily medication she required until a relative, together with his family moved in.

Regretfully six months later Mame died. It was early in the month of February 1987, and from that day, each morning when we opened our door, we would discover five of Mame's cats sitting on our doorstep, covered in snow and meowing for food and shelter. They appeared to be begging us to adopt them.

We believed since having lost their loving owners, and we, obviously being familiar faces, they must have perceived us to be their salvation. We of course, being animal lovers, had no hesitation in taking them in, to care for them until the end of their days.

Chapter 28

It was a sunny Saturday afternoon in August of 1988 we received a telephone call from daughter Shelly, who was at a 'horse and tack' auction at Acklington, having gone there to purchase a new bridle for her horse.

Wyn answered the phone, "Hello, Kennels and Cattery."

"It's me, mum - have you got any money?" said daughter Shelly.

"Why?" said Wyn

"You've bought a Shetland pony," replied Shelly

"A pony?" answered Wyn

"Yes," said Shelly, "Are you sitting down?"

Wyn hesitatingly asked "Why?"

"It's got a six week old foal," replied Shelly,

"Oh Mum I had to buy them because the meat man was

bidding for them."

It was not the £180 that bothered Wyn; it was the fact she had to go all the way up to Acklington on one of her busiest days in the kennels, as being school summer holidays they were full to capacity. Wyn left the staff in charge, and travelled to the mart with the money, and then arranged for the mare and foal to be transported to our paddock.

Carly the mother, was a little palomino Shetland pony, Dundee her six-week-old offspring, was also a beautiful golden palomino colour and not much bigger than a large dog. Being so very young he was still suckling and followed his mum Carly like a shadow, they were inseparable and both delightful little ponies.

The next unexpected scenario was when Yvonne came to our house with two Saanen goat kids lying asleep on the back seat of her car; they were only a few weeks old and both brilliant white in colour.

"What on earth have you got there?" asked Wyn

"Oh, Mum, they were going to be slaughtered for an Indian Ramadan festival," replied Yvonne." I had to save them."

We named them Jack and Jill.

Jack unfortunately lived only until he was about two years old before succumbing to liver disease; Jill was a sweet gentle little pet, who lived until she was ten years old. However one morning we noticed her chest had swelled up to about twice its normal size. We immediately called the vet who diagnosed she must have been stung by either a wasp or a bee. He warned us goats are notorious for just giving up the will to live, as might happen in this case; sadly, he was correct in his prediction. Jill lay down and refused to eat. We could not even tempt her with her favourite food and she contracted pneumonia and faded away.

These were the first of many animals Wyn and I rescued over the years. The next animal we rescued was a young Doberman dog. I discovered him when I was taking two of our own standard poodles for their daily exercise; he was lying in a lay-by about half a mile from our house. Upon observing him I hurried back home, put our own dogs into the house and quickly ran back up the road with a collar and lead.

The dog, I noticed, was lying in the exact same position which I had seen him a few minutes previously. As I approached, he slowly lifted his head and wagged his tail, (or should I say stump), and after hesitating he timidly got to his feet and came to greet me. I was shocked by his condition; he was skeletal, with a thick yellow discharge streaming from his eyes and nose. I walked him home but fearful he may have an infectious virus, we placed him in the isolation kennels to be on the safe side.

We began to make enquiries by ringing all the local animal sanctuaries, pet rescue shelters and the police but no one had reported him missing so he had obviously been dumped. We nursed Dylan, as we called him, back to health, and decided to keep him. We assumed the reason he was unwanted was probably the fact he was very highly-strung and very very destructive, however being young, we guessed about nine months old, we persevered with him and he blossomed into a faithful loyal pet.

Our next rescue was a Rottweiler puppy. Wyn answered the phone one morning to a client who regularly boarded her Doberman dog at our kennels. The client said she had taken her dog for a run through fields behind Darras Hall early that morning and as she climbed out of her car, she observed a woman dumping a bundle into the grass before speeding away in her car.

Our customer's inquisitive Doberman ran up to the bundle, which turned out to be a Rottweiler pup, approximately ten weeks old. We surmised being the end of January he must have been an unwanted Christmas puppy. But what kind of heartless person would dump such a young puppy in freezing winter temperatures, (that day was particularly cold, being minus ten degrees) instead of seeking help from the many organisations at hand, or indeed contacting the breeder?

It is beyond comprehension, especially when Rottweiler puppies were selling for at least, £450 each. We knew our client's Doberman despised other dogs and even had to be muzzled when out walking, so because she could not take the pup home she requested we keep the pup at our kennels until he was re-homed.

However, when she arrived with this cuddly fat bundle, obviously well fed and well looked after, I immediately fell in love with him and after making enquiries with the police in case he had been stolen, which was negative, we decided to keep him. Wyn had reservations, knowing just how enormous he would grow. He did in fact grow to be one of the biggest Rottweilers we have ever seen, and towered above any of the Rottweilers we ever boarded in the kennels.

Chapter 29

At the beginning of January 1991, we were informed by the local council the old bridge which straddled the river Pont about a hundred yards down from our house, had to be demolished because it had a seven-ton weight limit, therefore had to be rebuilt to conform to European Standards.

The council commenced work by demolishing and removing the old bridge, before erecting a temporary 'Foot Bridge' designed for pedestrians only, thus allowing access across the river. This 'foot bridge' was constructed of thick, heavy, wooden railway sleepers attached to a frame of scaffolding poles, which were hammered and driven down into the riverbank.

Unfortunately, at the end of January, the country

suffered five days of incessant, torrential rain, which caused the River Pont to swell into a raging torrent. The rapid gushing force of the water regrettably dislodged the scaffolding poles, resulting in the 'foot bridge' collapsing into the river thus forming a dam. Then to exacerbate matters, a large tree was uprooted by the engorged river and was swept downstream to wedge firmly against the collapsed bridge; this of course reinforced the 'dam.'

We could only watch and wait in horror, as the river water perilously began to creep slowly towards our house. In no time at all it had reached our front door and began to ooze under the thresh into the house. We literally felt the carpets begin to move under our feet as Wyn and I frantically began to grab articles of personal value to take them safely upstairs out of harm's reach. However, we both felt helpless as we watched the water level rise, and could only wait and let nature take its course.

Then to my horror, I suddenly remembered that being mid winter, the horses and ponies were in the stables. Fearing they would be in a state of panic, I rushed out to rescue them. I had to wade through icy water, which by then, at the stable area was thigh high. How I found the strength to open the stable doors against the pressure of water I will never comprehend, although somehow, after frantically struggling, I succeeded. Nevertheless, upon opening each door, the confined horse rushed past me in a state of terror, so I then had to battle my way through the water to catch them, to enable me to lead them to the safety of another paddock, situated on higher ground. I felt as if I were living a nightmare, and was understandably relieved when the task was completed.

Fortunately, it was not much later than the floodwater began to subside, revealing the thick covering of foul smelling silt, which had saturated and water logged the carpets. It was only then we discovered the extent of the damage to items large and small, which thankfully were covered by our insurance. This was certainly not an experience I would wish to go through again.

Chapter 30

Although we had owned numerous horses over the years, Wyn had never had enough confidence to ride any of them, even though she gave practical assistance to Yvonne and Shelly by helping to groom, train and feed them. She also helped to load them into the wagon when going to shows, and would lend a hand to muck out the stables when necessary. However, she was always very apprehensive and nervous around them, so I was completely flabbergasted when at the age of 54 she stated she wanted to buy a horse for herself.

I honestly could not believe it, and thought she must be suffering from the side effects of going through the change of life; I was convinced it would only be a passing whim, but no, she was serious. Wyn said she just wanted a gentle hack to ride around our land, so Yvonne, although sceptical, agreed to help her mum select a suitable horse. In principle she thought the same as myself, surely, her mum was too old to start riding, but Wyn was unwavering.

After viewing several horses, they eventually found one which seemed to be appropriate. He was a red bay gelding, four years old and fifteen one hands high. He was a perfect gentleman named Bracken, and was quiet, gentle with a lovely temperament, and perfect for a novice rider. Wyn had observed Yvonne and Shelly riding over the years, therefore knew all the basics in theory, so began to put this knowledge into practice to teach herself to ride.

At the beginning Wyn had one or two unfortunate mishaps. One instance was when she was hacking Bracken along the road and he was suddenly startled by a huge passing wagon which suddenly braked, causing the air brakes to make an unfamiliar loud hissing sound. This troubled Bracken, and he threw his head up in alarm, which, regrettably whacked Wyn on the nose to subsequently produce two real shiny black eyes. Wyn looked like a panda and had to suffer remarks from acquaintances such as 'Have you walked into a door?' nudge nudge, wink wink, humorously suggesting physical abuse, although anyone who knows me knows I wouldn't stoop so low as to raise my hand to any woman let alone my wife. Undaunted Wyn persevered, until she was quite capable of trotting and cantering although she never ever had the courage to attempt a gallop.

One day Wyn decided to go out for a hack with Yvonne who was riding her lovely grey horse called Jade. They had only ridden about two miles when Yvonne who was in the lead, began to canter along a path which meandered though a field. Wyn who was following closely behind suddenly noticed Jade's back feet slip on a large greasy patch on the path. There was no time to take evasive action, as a split second later Bracken's front feet stepped onto the grease. His legs slipped beneath him and he collapsed down onto his knees therefore catapulting Wyn, who somersaulted through the air before crashing heavily on her back. She was shaken and could hardly move.

Panicking, Yvonne rode to a nearby farmhouse for help. She furnished them with my telephone number and asked if they would please ring to ask me to come immediately to assist. Upon receiving the message I was enormously worried and quickly jumped into the car to drive to the scene to give assistance. I supported Wyn, who was in a great deal of pain, then helped her into the car and drove without delay to hospital.

After examination, the ex-rays to her spine showed there was no permanent damage, and she was allowed home, although she was bedridden and suffered intense pain for a further two weeks. As the pain began to subside, she, slowly with the aid of crutches, was able to venture out of bed, but it was another four weeks, before she could walk again unaided. The entire area of Wyn's lower back from her waist right down to her knees was black and purple with bruising. However as soon as she had recovered, she insisted on riding again. She maintained it was not Bracken's fault, it had been a pure accident, and because he was such a sweet gentle horse, he would never deliberately throw her off.

Two years later, Wyn required a new pair of reins for Bracken, so attended a livestock horse and tack sale which was held once a month at Ponteland mart. Whilst there, Wyn decided, 'just out of curiosity,' to view the horses which were for sale and tethered in the stalls.

She could not help but notice a pony in a dreadful condition. The pony was almost skeletal and had obviously been wearing a foal slip around his head, which he must have outgrown. Consequently, it had become so tight, it had cut into his flesh leaving a deep weal around his muzzle. Wyn was extremely disturbed and came home distraught. She described his plight to me, and I instantly said, as she had hoped, "Take the money, go back and buy him."

Wyn immediately returned to the mart and watched as the pony was led into the selling ring, but understandably, in the state he was in no one offered a bid. Therefore Wyn followed the owner who was leading the pony back outside. She asked him what the reserve price was, and immediately offered to buy him for the asking price. The pony was loaded into a wagon and brought to our paddock, to meet our other horses, and to graze on the lush grass.

Xanthe, as Wyn called him, was an eighteen month old, dark brown, bay gelding, and bore a close resemblance to a New Forest pony. Not only was he emaciated, he was also riddled with lice, and although very friendly, he had obviously never been handled much as he was very nervous.

However, he was desperate for affection and responded to Wyn's kindness and loving attention, although it took quite a while for her to be able to lift up his legs to attend to his feet. Nevertheless, Wyn's perseverance shone through and she gained his confidence, and Xanthe developed into a loving responsive pony who was always motivated and willing to please.

With the help of daughters, Yvonne and Shelly, Xanthe was broken in when he reached the age of three, and was then ridden around our fields by Wyn, who unconditionally trusted him. Regrettably, after a few years, Wyn suddenly became allergic to horses, as a result when handling or grooming them, her eyes would become red and itchy and begin to water profusely, she would start to sneeze uncontrollably, and her nose would become so blocked up she could hardly breathe.

To her anguish, she decided in the best interest of her horses, it would be better to find them loving homes.

Wyn was determined she would never sell them, as this would mean she could not control their future. Who knows where they could end up?, they could even be transported to the Continent for meat, so consequently they both went out on loan, to loving riders, ensuring Wyn could happily keep in contact with them.

Horses being such large animals can be very dangerous, and over the years, Yvonne and Shelly have sustained many injuries, thankfully none of them serious. Firstly Shelly, when she was eight years old and riding pony at a riding school, who, unbeknown to us was quite wicked since his favourite party trick being, that, when cantering, was to put his head down almost to the ground, then suddenly stop, and buck the rider off. One day whilst Shelly was having a lesson on him, he performed his party trick; she fell off and regrettably suffered a broken arm although fortunately it was only hairline fracture and healed without any lasting side effects.

It was when Shelly was twelve, Jason, their first horse stood on her left foot with all his weight, then with his hoof planted firmly on top of her riding boot, he swivelled himself around, and being quite a heavy cob type horse, his weight consequently tore her big toe-nail clean out and she was left in excruciating pain.

One day at the riding school which we were operating one of our ponies, in fact our smallest pony called Jester was walking past Jason. Unexpectedly Jason lurched swiftly forward, grabbed Jester by his mane and would not let go. Whilst I was endeavouring to make Jason release his hold, he abruptly turned and with mouth gaping open, showing huge teeth, he pitched forward and seized me by the chest, and then with a mouthful of, fortunately, only my jacket and jumper, he lifted me up into the air and shook me like a rag doll before dropping me.

'I told him he was a naughty boy.!!!!'

Yvonne often competed in British Show Jumping Affiliated shows; and it was at one event Dolly, her horse, bolted without warning, Yvonne had to fight with all her strength to bring her back under control; however, she only just managed to stop her within a few feet from a stone wall. Yvonne was quite traumatised when she glanced over the wall and saw there was a sheer drop of about fifty feet into a quarry. Yvonne realised if she had been unable to stop her, Dolly, being a show jumper would have just popped over the wall. It does not bear thinking about the consequences.

Several years later, Rolex, another horse belonging to Yvonne, suddenly reared up onto her hind legs and stamped down heavily onto Yvonne's foot, regrettably breaking two of her toes. This horse was predominantly a nasty piece of work, being a very bad tempered stroppy mare. When Yvonne was at work, and unable to feed the horses, the responsibility lay with me to carry out the chore. Consequently one day when I walked into Rolex's stable carrying her bucket of food, her ears went flat back onto her head in a threatening manner, she trapped me into a corner, turned her back on me, then lashed out with both back hooves. Thankfully, as my reflexes were good I managed to move quickly, but despite that, she caught me a glancing blow on the top of my thigh resulting in a hefty bruise. Another time Rolex head butted me, splitting the bridge of my nose wide open. I drove to the doctors' surgery for a tetanus injection and upon seeing the wound, the nurse said I needed butterfly stitches. She asked what had happened, and when I explained to her, she said, "I'm afraid the horse has broken your nose its all out of shape."

I laughed and said, "No, it's been out of shape for years."

Another scary moment, this time for Shelly who, at the time was riding her horse Rameses, through the main road, in the village of Ryton.

Rameses had always been bomb proof in traffic and safe even in the heaviest of traffic, but unfortunately a passing car backfired and Rameses frantically bolted. He was blindly galloping full speed amid cars, wagons and buses. Shelly battled hard to bring him to a halt, but had to pull so hard that Rameses' metal shoes caused a trail of sparks to fly behind as he skidded to a halt. Eventually he calmed down and strolled home as if nothing had happened.

Chapter 31

During the last few years in which I was physically plastering, I began to suffer badly with severe pains in both my elbows, consequently after diagnosis, I was proved to be suffering with arthritis, and I therefore had to have steroid injections, which were administered by a doctor at the local hospital. Regrettably the arthritis began to spread, firstly to my back, then to my neck, my legs and my ankles.

However I struggled on hoping to work as long as possible; nevertheless, plastering being such a hard occupation I was forced to retire, at the age of fifty-five.

From the day I retired from plastering and not wanting to sit on my backside all day, I began to help Wyn with the running of the boarding kennels.

I was soon to find that the managing of boarding kennels and cattery, apart from being a very rewarding profession, is also a very responsible line of business. It involves having to continuously ensure the animals, all of whom were much loved family pets, were correctly cared for, and to take the responsibility of administering, when necessary, medication. To feed in the manner they were accustomed to, to keep the pets clean and to exercise the dogs by walking them twice daily. This line of occupation means giving caring attention, not only twenty-four seven but seven fifty two.

As a result, we had been deprived of a holiday, or even a weekend break, for more than eighteen years; therefore Wyn and I decided we undoubtedly needed a well-earned vacation.

Several years earlier I had decided to give Wyn a surprise treat, and since Wyn had never ever flown before, I arranged for her to experience the joys of flying, by booking a one-hour pleasure flight in a Cessna aeroplane from Newcastle airport. Wyn was very tentative about the flight so I tried to reassure her, by relating from my own experiences, telling her flying was great and she would love it.

Unfortunately, during the flight, the small plane was frequently hitting pockets of turbulence, which caused it to suddenly drop a number of times. This truly scared

Wyn, and she was in fact very tense and extremely anxious. Then coming in to land, as we approached the airport, the plane appeared to be scarcely moving and simply hovering. This convinced Wyn the engine had stalled; she truly believed we would surely fall to the ground. Unfortunately, this experience undoubtedly made Wyn afraid of flying again, so we decided to take a holiday on a cruise liner.

We arranged to take the holiday at the beginning of March 1993. We chose that month since it, being in between Christmas and Easter holidays, meant it was usually one of the quietest months of the year for the kennels. We consequently closed the business for two weeks, and arranged for Ben and Polly to stay at our house, to care for our own animals. Accordingly, we booked a cruise with the Fred Olsen line, sailing on the 5th March, selecting an outside cabin on one of the higher decks on their ship the Black Watch, and were relatively excited, as we travelled by train to Southampton.

We, together with other passengers, were met at the train station by a courtesy bus, which drove us to the collecting lounge at the quayside, where everyone was served with free hot drinks and snacks, until it was time to embark. It was five o'clock p.m when the ship finally sailed from port, to an organised champagne pool party; everyone drank free champagne and as the music played, the passengers danced around the outside swimming pool as the shore slowly disappear from the horizon. The cruise's itinerary was to visit the Canary Isles, making several ports of call on the way, including Spain. Madeira, and Agidir, in Morocco.

We soon became friends with several passengers, and when we arrived at Agidir, Wyn and I decided to go ashore with a group of six of our new acquaintants. The eight of us decided to wander around together, when suddenly, a young Arab teenager, who spoke perfect English, approached us, and offered to guide us around the area. He said he would accompany us to the nearby Old City.

We promptly agreed, imagining it must surely be a contrast to the usual tourist sightseeing locations; the young Arab informed us his brother was a chemist, who owned a shop in the old city bazaar, so we agreed for him to escort us to the location.

The Bazaar was an area cluttered with old junk; we were amused and could not comprehend how anybody could possibly buy any of the items on the stalls. Amongst the rubbish were old worn out threadbare tyres, broken rusty bikes, old ragged clothes and broken pots, the whole place resembled a scrap yard.

The chemist shop was an open fronted stall, filled to capacity with bottles, jars, sacks and boxes. The chemist was very friendly and pleasant, and insisted we sit down whilst he made us a cup of Arabic tea, which, when ready, he served to us in small glasses. This brought back

fond memories of my army service in North Africa. As we drank the tea, the banter commenced, we enquired about the potions and lotions, and the chemist pointed to one jar and said, "That one is an aphrodisiac."
Chuckling, the wife of one our friends piped up "You'd better give my husband a pound of that."
Another quipped, "My husband will need a stone."

The Chemist informed us he also had a slimming remedy; this 'remedy' resembled thin twigs, which had to be boiled for two hours, after which the residual liquid would be drank after it has cooled down. There was no way Wyn or I could be persuaded to buy it, no thanks, there are plenty of trees in our own garden.

Another port of call during the cruise was Lisbon, Portugal; as usual, a private bus dropped us off in a square in the centre of town, and it was arranged for the passengers to converge back at the same place, at three o'clock to be bussed back to the ship. After wandering around and looking at several places of interest, which included an ancient ornate palace. Wyn and I began to stroll around the town centre, window-shopping. Unexpectedly we came upon a beautiful shiny black carriage to which was harnessed a pair of fine-looking chestnut horses, which was obviously used to drive tourists around the town. The driver noticed Wyn videoing the horses, so began to hassle us, pleading with us to take a trip around the town; we explained we had to be back at the prearranged picking up point at three o'clock, and consequently time was limited. He replied in broken English "Yes, yes, I understand, plenty time."

We climbed into the carriage and settled ourselves down onto the red velvet seat, to enjoy the pleasant ride in the warm sunshine, and were captivated by the wonderful scenery we encountered throughout our trip. However, after a while, I looked down at my watch and perceived it was almost three o'clock.

I leant forward, tapped the driver on the shoulder and pointed to my watch, therefore realising time was running out, he nodded, shook the reins, clicked his tongue and sent the horses into a canter.

Because it was normal practice for the horses to just lazily amble along, they were quite perturbed and became anxious and agitated at being forced to canter over the uneven cobbled streets.

Unpredictably, without warning, one of the harness straps, which was fixed around the horses tails, suddenly snapped, and as a result, the horse being so stressed out, lifted his tail up into the air and blasted out projectile diarrhoea. His aim was perfect, not only the driver, but also Wyn and myself were sprayed from head to toe with strands of khaki coloured shit, which tangled through our hair; and splattered, not only over our faces, but also peppered over all our clothing. We looked at each other, and upon seeing, the nauseating state we were in, were reduced to a fit of giggles.

The driver brought the carriage to a halt and climbed

down. His face was deadpan serious, not a flicker of a smile, he was full of remorse and extremely apologetic. We assured him it was okay and Wyn offered him a handful of paper handkerchiefs, so the three of us proceeded to clean ourselves up as best as we could.

We were in fact about fifteen minutes late for the bus which was waiting patiently for us. However as we climbed up the steps, the passengers started to grab their noses and shout, "Ugh what's that disgusting smell?" Upon noticing the state we were in, they enquired, "What on earth has happened to you two?"

They began to split their sides laughing when we explained. I think the whole ship must have heard about our escapade, as we were the butt of their jokes for days.

Two years later, we had our second cruise, this time on the P&O's cruise liner the Canberra. Since Wyn suffers from motion sickness, even though the sea was calm, on the second day of the cruise she became ill and we had to call the doctor to administer an anti seasickness injection. The doctor was a Scotsman who told us he had sailed on cruise ships for years, and was very surprised Wyn was nauseous, he joked. "The water is like a mill pond. It's a good job you were not on the last December cruise. We sailed through a force eleven gale and I had to treat many passengers for injuries, including two broken arms, one broken leg, and to boot, a lady passenger was thrown so violently against a table her ear was almost completely torn off and I had to stitch it back on, which was almost impossible as I was being thrown from side to side."

This was another fabulous holiday, where one of the ports of call was at the Cape Verde' Islands which are off the coast of West Africa. We were given to understand it was the first time a cruise ship had ever called at that destination, and since the Island did not have any facilities for docking such a huge ship as the Canberra, we had to anchor out at sea and the ship's tenders (lifeboats) transported the passengers to the island.

The welcome from the natives was exceptionally hospitable; they were dancing and singing on the dock to welcome the passengers, whom they believed would bring much sought after trade to their poor existence.

Since there were not enough taxis to cope with the surplus of people, the islanders had commandeered some rickety, old, open topped wagons, and had equipped them with wooden benches, to serve as makeshift seats, thus enabling the ship's passengers to be transport into the town centre.

Although some of the passengers, especially female, were dressed up to the nines and wearing very expensive designer clothes, we didn't hear anyone complain, as they scrambled up into the back of the wagons to take their seats on the wobbly old benches. Everyone seemed to take it in good humour and since it was so novel, it added to the fun.

However, shortly after we were put ashore, the sea became very choppy, and intensified to such an extent it was obvious, by the large swell, it was becoming more treacherous by the minute. We were informed our lifeboat was the very last one to leave the ship, before the captain, after contemplating the weather conditions, decided the sea was too rough and too perilous to attempt any more crossings.

But where did that leave us we wondered? Wyn, I, along with six boatloads of passengers had to make the voyage back to the ship.

Subsequently, after earnest consultation with the captain of the Canberra, the lifeboat crew decided we should attempt the return crossing; therefore, the passengers climbed into the lifeboats and set off. This in itself was incredibly daunting, as the huge swell whipped the waves high above our boat before crashing down onto passengers and crew alike, soaking us through to the skin.

The crew made numerous attempts to drop us off at the Canberra's landing stage, but each time we neared the ship, it became much too hazardous, as the risk of our lifeboat, colliding with the Canberra seemed imminent. We would therefore have to veer quickly away, drive around once more, and come in yet again for another attempt. Thankfully, we eventually made it, drenched, but safe and being the optimists we are, we just thought of it as yet another adventure to remember.

Chapter 32

Over the last few years, we began to think it was essential to consider retiring as Wyn had run the kennels for twenty years, and was certainly feeling the need to relax. In addition, my arthritis was worsening and I myself was finding it more and more exhausting to maintain the kennels and cattery buildings, which, together with the stables, seemed to be forever in need of one repair or another. It was becoming more challenging for me to keep the fences in good order, to ensure the horses were safely enclosed; it was beyond doubt, very hard to say the least.

I had endured severe pain, and worked for numerous years with the discomfort of haemorrhoids. At the onset of the problem, I was prescribed various treatments, but since none of them ever seemed to ease the pain and discomfort, the doctor referred me to a specialist at the Newcastle Royal Victoria Infirmary. There, I had the haemorrhoids injected, although this was extremely unpleasant, it relieved the pain for a period of time, but unfortunately, after a while, they came back with a vengeance. The specialist suggested that I should have surgery, to finally remove them. I was extremely apprehensive, but also desperate for relief, so after hesitating, I finally agreed. It was a few weeks later I received the dreaded letter; a bed was available.

On the day of admission, Wyn packed me an overnight bag and drove me to the hospital, whereupon arriving at the ward; the duty nurse showed me to a bed and said I was allowed one meal before the nil by mouth order came into force. She left my bedside, and then a moment later reappeared with the lunch menu. I scanned through it, only to discover there was no vegetarian food listed. The nurse said she was sorry but there was nothing else available, so after some deliberation, Wyn and I decide to make our way to the hospital restaurant, where I found I was able to select from a number of vegetarian dishes on offer on the menu. When I arrived back at the ward, the nurse kindly offered me a cheese sandwich. I had to decline, explaining I had just eaten in the restaurant, and could not consume another mouthful. However I thanked her for being so thoughtful.

Shortly afterwards, the anaesthetist who was to tend

me in the operating theatre during my operation, arrived at my bedside to take a phial of blood. It was whilst chatting he said I was his first patient, which of course didn't instil me with confidence.

An hour or so later he came back, looking sheepish, and said he needed to take another blood sample, as he had forgotten to label the first phial of blood.

Two hours later, another doctor, a woman this time, came to chat about the operation and to take me through the whole procedure. After explaining the course of action, she said, "It's obligatory, I have to warn you of the risks of the operation. There is a chance that you might be left incontinent, and as a result, would have to wear nappies for the rest of your life."

My stomach dropped like a lead weight, my mind boggled with visions of myself waddling around in giant nappies, I said, "No way, I would rather suffer with haemorrhoids. I'm certainly not going to have the operation, if there is even a remote chance of that."
She seemed taken aback and left my bedside, a few minutes later, the specialist himself, a Mr Campbell, came and sat on the edge of my bed, "What's this, I hear you've changed you mind about the operation?" he said.
"I'm sorry but there is no way I'm going to go through with it if it means I might be left incontinent." I replied.
He reassured me by saying he, personally, would carry out the operation. He spoke quietly, and went on to say he could guarantee there wouldn't be any nasty side

effects. Feeling slightly more confident, I half-heartedly agreed to allow the operation to take place, but needless to say, I did not get much sleep that night.

It was later the next afternoon when still full of trepidation, I was wheeled to theatre to go through the operation, which I am very relieved to say was successful.

I was still slightly sedated, and 'dazed', when at two o'clock in the morning; I woke to find myself in darkness and in an alien environment, feeling incredibly anxious I began stumbling about the ward like a zombie, shouting "Wyn, where are you? Wyn."
The night nurse quickly came to my rescue, she took me by the arm and escorted me back to bed, saying "Come on Ron, you're in hospital, remember?"
Settling me back into bed, she plumped up the pillows and asked, "Would you like a nice cup of tea?"
I nodded, as I was gasping for a drink. My throat was dry as a stick and my mouth felt like a sewer. The tea was served hot and milky and was greatly appreciated.
Two days later the doctor allowed me to go home, saying the wound should heal within about two weeks. He wrote out a prescription for painkillers with instructions to take when required.

Maybe the wound would have healed in that specified time, but unbeknown to myself, I had contracted the dreaded hospital bug. This bug seemed to be resistant to all the normal antibiotics, which were prescribed, so consequently the wound took an unbelievable six months to heal. During that period going to the loo was excruciatingly painful, it felt almost as though I was passing razor blades and since the insufferable agony persisted for such a lengthy period, it was ages before I could admit I was glad I had had the operation.

I am now free from the embarrassing problem which had plagued me for years, and as time is a great healer, the pain is now a distant memory.

It was at the beginning of November 2000, the whole country suffered from unrelenting, torrential rain; consequently, several counties were severely flooded. Because of our previous experience of flooding we were very worried. However we thought we had escaped the worst of the severe weather, when suddenly on the 6th of November, the whole area of Ponteland, experienced the worst flooding in living memory, as the main street became submerged under at least two feet of floodwater.

The river Pont became a rampant torrent, and as it rose above its banks, the water began to progressively creep closer to our property. We frantically rang the council requesting help, and they very kindly rushed to our aid, by providing, and stacking sandbags around the doors to our house, and cattery. Wyn firmly believed, sandbagging would mean we would be safe from flooding, but I advised her no mater how many sandbags were stacked around our property, if the river water reached us, we would in fact, definitely flood. I was fully geared up, and told myself "I'm not going to be caught out this time,"

Therefore having had plenty of warning, I moved the horses to the paddock, on a higher level, before the floodwater reached the stable area.

It was, five o'clock in the afternoon Wyn, who at the time was on the telephone in the hall, felt the carpet move under her feet, glancing down, she noticed the carpet was undulating. She yelled for me to come, nevertheless we could only look on powerless, as our thoughts screamed, "Oh no! Not again."

We watched in horror as the water quickly rose to a height of about ten inches - so much for sand bags.

The water rapidly seeped into the electric points above the skirting boards, cutting the power off and leaving us in total darkness; the comparable scenario occurred with the telephone connections. Our very first thoughts were for the several cats, which were being boarded in our cattery. These of course needed to be rescued, as by then, the water had risen to at least two feet high in the cattery building.

Being extremely concerned, we instantly called the fire service for help, (thank God for mobile phones). We explained the situation, and even though the roads were closed, due to the extreme high levels of floodwater, the fire engines arrived within fifteen minutes. The firemen were wonderfully obliging and caring, and although by then, the water in the cattery was thigh high, they waded in to rescue the cats. They carefully extracted each one from its compartment, placed them into carrying cages, which we had provided, then waded back to our house, to take the cats to the safety of our upstairs bedrooms.

This flood was especially dreadful; since amongst the many belongings, which we lost, were many family photos, and our complete video collection of holidays, parties, weddings, and Christmases- these items of course can never be replaced.

The filthy floodwater remained in the house for twenty-four hours, before slowly subsiding, leaving a muddy smelly residue. The insurance company offered to accommodate us in a hotel, until the house was habitable once again. However since our kitchen was on a higher level, and the bedrooms and bathroom being upstairs, meant they were not affected by the flood and as a result were uncontaminated; consequently we elected to stay at home. The reason being, we had the responsibility of caring for all our own animals and needed to be on hand. We opted to live this way, not realising it would take four long months to get back to normal. Firstly, it took six dehumidifiers, running continuously for twenty-four hours, and every day of the week, for six weeks before the house had dried out enough for the builders to commence work. They gutted the whole downstairs of the house, pulling up all the floorboards, and removing all the internal and external doors. They levered the skirting boards off, took the radiators off, and then hacked the plaster off the walls. They also ripped the downstairs cloakroom toilet suite out and removed all the wall and floor tiles until the house ended up resembling a bombsite. Finally, after four months of chaos, the work had been completed and the whole downstairs had been renewed and decorated to a high standard; in addition all our furniture, furnishings and carpets had been replaced.

The inconvenience and the unsociable hours of having to work seven days a week, every week of the year, including Christmas Day. Boxing Day, New Years Eve and New Years Day was starting to tell. A big minus for Wyn was having to suffer working outside in the severe cold conditions of mid winter; consequently, this surpassed the desire to continue.

Therefore, after twenty years of running the boarding kennels, although Wyn had thoroughly enjoyed it, the work was eventually beginning to take its toll on her, since it was Wyn who answered the telephone to take the bookings and her who answered the door to meet customers with their pets. This scenario meant she hardly ever sat down to an uninterrupted meal, and could never completely relax, as she was always at everyone's beck and call.

The extreme cases relating to these circumstances were, once, at half past eleven at night, we were asleep in bed, when the doorbell rang, and unbelievably it was a customer to collect his cat and dog. Wyn without complaint, got dressed and took him down to the kennels to collect his pets.

On yet another occasion, this time it was four thirty in the morning when the doorbell chimed. Wyn observing the time, was frantic with worry as she threw her clothes on, immediately thinking the worst, that something must be wrong with either Yvonne or Shelly, but incredibly when Wyn opened the door, she discovered it was a customer. "I've come to collect my cat," she said,
Wyn stared at her in disbelief, the woman explained, she had just got off a plane, and decided to come straight to the cattery from the airport, since living in the opposite direction meant it would save her from having to come back. Wyn again obliged, I am afraid I would have told her where to go.

After a lot of soul-searching we reluctantly agreed it was time to retire, so contacted an estate agent to place our house and business on the market. Wyn set in motion the search for a new house and decided a bungalow would most suitable seeing we weren't getting any younger. Wyn viewed several in the area before deciding on one on the Darras Hall Estate which she thought was appropriate, and even though it required a lot of work to update, it was exactly what we were looking for, it being detached with very private secluded gardens. We decided to make an offer, which was duly accepted.

In the meantime, we found a buyer for our property so the contracts were drawn up and signed and we moved on the second of November 2001.

I often reminisce and look back over the years, going through each stage of my life and appreciate the fact I have had an remarkably colourful life, and I'm truly thankful for all the kindness, help and advice shown to me in the past by, primarily my headmaster Mr Tweddle, and then Skipper Teasdale from Grainger Park Boys Club, also from John Fenwick of Fenwick's Department Store and then last but by no means least. Major Brindley my army Commanding Officer.

These vibrant memories keep me happy, and apart from the medical problems, which I now suffer from, I am content and undeniably grateful, I met Wyn, who gave birth to my two beautiful daughters who in turn, firstly. Shelly gave me two extremely handsome, considerate and very intelligent grandsons, Paul and David. (They take after their granddad of course), who are both studying at Newcastle University.

Then a gorgeous blonde, blue-eyed granddaughter. Amber, who is still at school and excelling in artwork, all three are, unquestionably, a credit to her.

Next, it was Yvonne's turn to give birth to my second granddaughter, Ashley, who is without doubt, another stunner. She is a blue-eyed blonde, with hair curling down to her waist. She is bright and intelligent, and now the proud owner of Wyn's pony, Xanthe. I am immensely proud of them all, and can categorically say, they are the light of my life.

Throughout my life, I have always been obsessively proud of being a Geordie, and hope I will be forgiven for being complacent about my achievements, since it is difficult to envisage me, that scruffy ragged little urchin Ronnie Jackson, from the dire poverty of Scotswood Road, now, after working so hard over the years, to finally arrive in the position of not having a mortgage or any debts.

To own a B.M.W car, and be the owner of twenty-five acres of prime land at Kirkley, to purchase a property, with cash, in one of the most prestigious and affluent areas in the North East, Darras Hall, which is the favoured area in which to reside, by famous top sportsmen, such as near neighbours, the outstanding, brilliant Newcastle United football stars, Alan Shearer and Peter Beardsley, and (I hope) enough money in the bank, to last until the end of my days.